Berlin

A guide to recent architecture

•••

Duane Phillips

Berlin

A guide to recent architecture

● ● ● ellipsis KÖNEMANN

•••

CREATED, EDITED AND DESIGNED BY
Ellipsis London Limited
55 Charlotte Road London EC2A 3QT
E MAIL ...@ellipsis.co.uk
www http://www.ellipsis.co.uk
PUBLISHED IN THE UK AND AFRICA BY
Ellipsis London Limited
SERIES EDITOR Tom Neville
EDITOR Helen Castle
SERIES DESIGN Jonathan Moberly
LAYOUT Pauline Harrison

COPYRIGHT © 1997 Könemann
Verlagsgesellschaft mbH
Bonner Str. 126, D-50968 Köln
PRODUCTION MANAGER Detlev Schaper
PRINTING AND BINDING Sing Cheong
Printing Ltd
Printed in Hong Kong

ISBN 3 89508 634 7 (Könemann)
ISBN 1 899858 03 2 (Ellipsis)

Duane Phillips 1997

Contents

Introduction: memories

How does one convey the sense of a time and place that no longer exist? How does one explain the forces of history and transition? How can one imagine the memories of another?

The two Berlins that I have known since 1980 no longer exist. Gone is their *raison d'être*. Gone is the concrete structure that determined the social, political and economic forces unique to the divided city.

Many cities have easily distinguishable districts, each with its own characteristics. Berlin had these as well until 9 November 1989. Then, overnight, Berlin gained a new district. One without parallel anywhere in the world, a district 100 metres wide, without trees, without buildings, without sound, snaking its way through the very heart of the city.

This new district, the former death strip, is rapidly disappearing. Slowly, surely, the two Berlins are merging. Soon, this district will no longer exist. In future editions of this guide it will not appear. It will itself become another memory.

In order to understand what one sees and remembers, one needs to understand the reasons why. In order to communicate this, I have included background material in the description of the individual projects. Through the cumulative effect, readers will gain an understanding of the why.

In selecting the projects I have used three time frames to define 'recent architecture'. The first is for those projects finished before or planned in the mad scramble of 1990/91 and now completed. The second is for the second wave of projects now under construction and set for completion in 1997. The third is for those projects that have resulted from major competitions and planning studies, a watch-this-space. I have included these in order to allow readers to return to the site some time in the future and to remember how it was before.

Through the guide, I hope to give readers their own memories of a Berlin in transition; of a Berlin physically growing together but psychologically growing apart; of a Berlin being pushed, pulled and dragged into the twenty-first century by forces it does not understand and is not prepared to encounter.

CHRONOLOGY

1237	Berlin founded
1712–86	Friedrich the Great
1781–1841	Karl Friedrich Schinkel
1871	German Unification (Bismarck)
1914–18	World War 1
1919–33	Weimar Republic (Bauhaus)
1933	Hitler assumes power
1939–45	World War 2
1945	Berlin and Germany each divided into four sectors (American, British, French, Soviet)
1948–49	currency reform in Western sectors. Soviets seal off access to West Berlin. Western Allies supply West Berlin by air
1949	founding of West Germany (American, British and French sectors) with Bonn as provisional capital until such time as Berlin's status is 'normalised'
1949	founding of East Germany (Soviet sector) with East Berlin as capital. Status of West Berlin remains that of an occupied city, technically not part of either West or East Germany
1953	uprising of building workers in Stalin Allee, East Berlin. Put down by Soviet tanks

Berlin: a guide to recent architecture

1957	Interbau Building Exhibition in West Berlin
1961	construction of Berlin Wall around West Berlin
1972	treaty defining West Berlin's status signed, allows limited travel between East and West Berlin
1984–87	International Building Exhibition (*Internationale Bauausstellung 1984 – IBA*) in West Berlin
1989	9 November, fall of Berlin Wall
1991–95	Berlin building boom spurred by tax incentives
1996–	recession hits, office rents collapse, many projects aborted or abandoned due to over-supply
1999–2000	proposed date for governmental move from Bonn to Berlin

DEFINITIONS

Certain terms have come to dominate the language of architecture in Berlin. For those not familiar with them, a selection is provided here.

Blockrandbebauung the act of building along the street edge, leaving the block's interior open as green space

Gründerzeit a term referring to the years 1871–1914, typified by *Mietshäuser* (see below)

IBA the International Building Exhibition, 1984–87. This consisted of two parts: New Build organised by Professor Josef P Kleihues, and Old Build headed by Professor Hardt-Waltherr Hämer. The primary goal of New Build was to reinstate the Berlin block as the primary urban element through *Blockrandbebauung*. The primary aim of Old Build was to repair and modernise the block's interior (mostly

Berlin: a guide to recent architecture

through self-help by the residents) and to place needed social infrastructure (parks, day-care centres, etc) in the gaps left by destroyed buildings

Lochfassade a façade of holes, usually in a vertical format. Where appropriate the façade is clad in stone and the windows are nothing more than a series of vertical openings, punched out of the solid, imitating the *Mietshäuser*

Mietshäuser typical Berlin apartment blocks built between 1871 and 1914, typified by *Lochfassade*, a 22-metre eaves height (dictated by fire codes), as well as wings and courtyard buildings, sometimes five deep in the block

ACKNOWLEDGEMENTS

Thank you to Silvia, Frank and all the architectural firms who have supplied us with information. Extra-special thanks go out to Tom Neville and the amazing Armelle Tardiveau who have made this project possible.

Thank yous also to Peter Cook, Christine Hawley and the late Ron Herron – I realise only now how fortunate I was to have had them as tutors at the AA – and to Rem Koolhaas who inspired me to come to Europe in the first place.

I also wish to extend a thank you to that unknown East German borderguard in his observation tower, who, at midnight, was tapping his machine gun to the sound of David Bowie, during a transvestite circus performance at Tempodrom in Potsdamer Platz in 1980. At that surreal moment, I fell in love with Berlin.

DP January 1997

TO DEREK

Using this book

Seven years have passed and for most Berliners, the wall still exists mentally, dividing the city into East and West.

Both Berlins had their own centres, their own easts, wests, norths, and souths based upon historical districts. This book is organised to reflect this, helping to give the visitor an understanding of the developments now taking place, and of the projects that are starting to physically (re)unite the two Berlins.

The selections are, where possible, sequenced into a walking tour, or in a way that allows easy, direct connections to be made by bus or U-Bahn.

We have given the coordinates for each entry based on the Falk Map of Berlin. Beware: street and station names are constantly changing in the eastern part of the city.

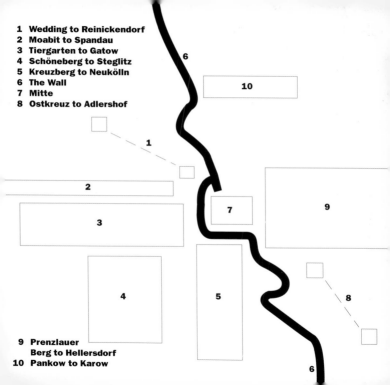

1 Wedding to Reinickendorf
2 Moabit to Spandau
3 Tiergarten to Gatow
4 Schöneberg to Steglitz
5 Kreuzberg to Neukölln
6 The Wall
7 Mitte
8 Ostkreuz to Adlershof

9 Prenzlauer
  Berg to Hellersdorf
10 Pankow to Karow

Wedding to Reinickendorf

Library at Luisenbad

One of the most successful urban design projects recently built in Berlin. This programme involves the restoration, conversion and integration of a listed building ensemble into a new multilevel library. The new library itself is a two-storey structure with its main floor at basement level. The interior space is exciting and has good natural lighting despite its orientation.

The scale remains small, the interventions careful; and the historical courtyard remains intact. The idea of designing the new as an extension of the existing *ad hoc* ensemble is logical and correct.

The site has long been a neglected ruin. This project has become a much-used and enjoyed faciltiy for the local community.

ADDRESS Badstraße 35–36, Berlin-Wedding [P–14]
CLIENT Land Berlin, Hochbauamt Wedding
STRUCTURAL ENGINEER Professor Manleitner, Hr Becker
COST DM 24 million
SIZE 2651 square metres
U-BAHN Osloer Straße/Pankstraße
BUS 328
ACCESS open

Chestnutt und Neiss 1996

Chestnutt und Neiss 1996

Youth centre, Demminer Straße

An existing cube has been wrapped with stairs and terraces. The pitched roof is gone. Now a terrace, it is an occupied space. This building invites young people to meet here and take it over, both inside and out and from top to bottom.

The interior has been only partly reorganised. The main stair is centrally located and the exterior terraces and stairs double as the required second means of escape. The exterior has been clad in rich brick-work; the size of the window openings reflects the uses and importance of the rooms behind.

ADDRESS Demminer Straße 28, Berlin-Wedding [Q–12]
CLIENT Bezirksamt Wedding
STRUCTURAL ENGINEER Ing. Büro für Statik + Baukonstruktion Lorenz Limnhoff
COST DM 3.67 million
SIZE 2367 square metres gross
S-BAHN Voltastraße
BUS 120
ACCESS open

Hans Kollhoff 1988

Wedding to Reinickendorf

Hans Kollhoff 1988

Point houses

This is a project which sticks to the rules and then breaks them. The normal 22-metre eaves line is not respected here. The architect has placed two white towers containing the flats away from the firewall, using the vertical circulation space to separate yet tie in the existing house with the new. Attached but not adjacent, the towers on their spindly legs clearly have their own character and identity, separate from their neighbours.

There is no underground parking. Instead, cars can be driven between the legs and into the planted courtyard. If necessary, the fire department can also continue into the second courtyard where the children's playground is located.

The concept is clean and simple, as are the buildings. They are a refreshing example of how something with quality can be built on a low budget.

ADDRESS Grüntaler Straße 57, Berlin-Wedding [Q–14]
CLIENT Daphine Grundstücksgesellschaft GmbH + Co
COST DM 3.8 million
SIZE 1960 square metres
S-BAHN Wollankstraße
TRAM 23, 24
BUS 227, 255
ACCESS open

Carlos Zwick 1993

Carlos Zwick 1993

Offices, Jacobsenweg

Set within a conservation area of brick industrial buildings, this small new office building has been able both to fulfil its function successfully and to be respectful of its neighbours.

As a part of the site limitations, the existing brick wall along the street was restored as an independent structure. The new three-storey building was set back approximately 2 metres, but connected to the wall by a glazed corridor which serves as the access to the ground-floor offices. The main entrance is slightly curved to accentuate the spiral staircase behind. The upper floors have a central spine, allowing offices to look on to either the street or the courtyard.

The brick detailing, including the cornice, is immaculate. The architects have obviously studied Berlin's rich prewar industrial architecture and have created an almost perfect 1920s building. Rather than becoming dated, it should serve in years to come as a benchmark for sensitivity and quality.

Wedding to Reinickendorf

ADDRESS Jacobsenweg 41, Berlin-Reinickendorf [L–16]
STRUCTURAL ENGINEER Manfred Baumann
SIZE 290 square metres
U-BAHN Holzhauser Straße
BUS 125, 322
ACCESS open

Claus Peter Claussen 1989

Claus Peter Claussen 1989

Office and workshop, JAC 63

Jewels are usually found in unexpected places. This is no exception. Situated in a conservation area of brick industrial buildings, the architects have successfully integrated two new buildings into the existing fabric through careful placement and use of materials.

The client, a stone mason, required new offices, a workshop, and a delivery yard. In the tradition of this area, the new office block was located towards the street, placed on the end of the site to act as the extended edge of the conservation area. The new workshop was positioned at the back of the site, creating the rear edge of the new courtyard.

The office building – containing an exhibition space, a flat and a sculptor's studio – uses a concrete-skeleton system and a massive brick wall to the street acts as a heat-storage wall.

The workshop building is conceived as a reinforced, precast-concrete system spanning between two massive brick end walls. The south façade is almost entirely clad with light steel panels.

Taken as a whole, the logical placement of different functions and excellent handling of materials combine to produce a refined, restrained composition which is well integrated with its surroundings.

ADDRESS Jacobsenweg 63, Berlin-Wittenau [L–16]
CLIENT B u M Gebauer
LANDSCAPE ARCHITECT Stephan Haan
STRUCTURAL ENGINEER Franz Hille
COST offices DM 3.08 million; workshop DM 940,000
SIZE offices 809 square metres; workshop 531 square metres
U-BAHN Holzhauser Straße
BUS 322, 125
ACCESS open

Backmann und Schieber 1992

Backmann und Schieber 1992

Hotel and office complex, An der Mühle

This forgotten corner of Berlin-Tegel has been creatively readapted through restoration, conversion and a series of additions into a picturesque ensemble.

An existing mill complex, connected by water to the main harbour, was vacant and derelict. As part of the IBA (International Building Exhibition, 1984–87), the area had been extensively analysed and proposals for housing and cultural institutions were worked up. It was foreseen that this would be an attractive location for offices and a hotel due to its waterside site and its proximity to the autobahn, Tegel airport and the main shopping street to the south.

The mill's exterior has been restored and the building, along with the flour-storage and the boiler houses, has been converted into offices.

The silo has been converted into a hotel through the gutting of the interior and the careful incision of small square windows into the façade. The window detailing gives the impression that they are actually holes in the wall, preserving the industrial character of the building. A modern steel and mirrored-glass hotel extension has been placed to the west to act as the edge of the complex. The restored former official's residence serves as luxury suites for the hotel.

New three-storey buildings respecting the mill's eaves height have been placed to the south and east, enclosing the complex and giving it a sense of intimacy and protection. A six-storey office cube with a round silo-type element on the roof acts as a visual marker for the different site axes within the complex and from the area. Brick cladding helps to tie them into the complex despite the somewhat simple detailing.

The careful placement of the new *vis-à-vis* the old has helped to ensure the success of the urban design. Still, something is lacking: it is a bit cold, a bit too sterile. Maybe it's too cleaned-up; maybe it needed to incorporate

Steinebach & Weber 1992

Steinebach & Weber 1992

some housing in order to bring it to life.

This is a problem typical of industrial buildings that have been converted for commercial use: the atmosphere gets lost in the translation. However, taking the scheme as a whole, the architects can only be praised for their adaptive reuse and careful placing of new elements, which have combined to create a beautiful oasis out of derelict fragments.

ADDRESS An der Mühle 5–9, Berlin-Tegel [K–17]
CLIENT Ernst Freiberger
STRUCTURAL ENGINEER Hildebrandt & Sieber GmbH
CONSERVATION OFFICER Professor Helmut Engel, Wolf-Borwin Wendlandt
COST DM 70 million
SIZE offices 15,000 square metres gross; 125-room hotel
U-BAHN Alt-Tegel
BUS 224
ACCESS open

Steinebach & Weber 1992

Steinebach & Weber 1992

Moabit to Spandau

Bundespräsidialamt

Until reunification, the symbolic home of the federal president was the Schloß Bellevue. With its grand function rooms and official guest accommodation, it was perfectly suited for its ceremonial role. The only problem was that the federal president resided for the greater part of the year in Bonn, thus the building was significantly under used.

With reunification, the then president, Richard von Weizecker, decided to make a significant gesture by declaring that he and his staff would move back to Berlin, East Berlin. Various buildings along the Unter den Linden were considered, but in the end rejected due to security restrictions and space requirements.

An extension to the Schloß Bellevue was proposed as the answer and an Europewide competition was organised. The winner proposed a simple elliptical form, located a short distance away from the existing building. The rounded edges avoid the problem of axial relationships within the park; instead the extension fits in unobtrusively among the trees.

The building itself is divided between an outer ring and an inner core, with internal bridges linking the two. A potentially exciting space, but only a privileged few will experience it.

ADDRESS Spreeweg, Berlin-Tiergarten [N-10]
S-BAHN Bellevue
BUS 100, 187
STATUS under construction

Moabit to Spandau

Gruber + Kleine-Kraneburg

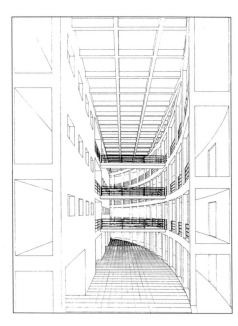

Gruber + Kleine-Kraneburg

Spreebogen complex

When the milling industry vacated their premises along the River Spree, they left behind an architectural legacy of warehouses, silos and mills. Few of these buildings were considered reusable by modern industry. Property developers like those in London Docklands, however, soon discovered just how desirable the water's edge could be and how cheaply the land could be obtained. Unlike Docklands, though, this site is centrally located.

A new development concept was proposed which included the demolition of most buildings, though some were spared and integrated with the new buildings and the new river promenade.

The first of the new office complexes completed was what has now become known as 'Teleport', a series of six-storey towers linked by two-storey connections, clad in large precast-compound-concrete panels with cast-in terracotta tiles. Although the architects, Ganz + Rolfes, have tried to integrate their buildings with the remaining industrial buildings through the use of red terracotta, the scale of the concrete panels prevents a successful relationship. Overall the complex is dense and overpowering, and the atmosphere sterile and empty.

A very different effect has been achieved in the renovation and addition to the old dairy. This brick building dates from 1864, and had been converted and extended over the years until it reached a length of over 100 metres. Now converted by the architect W R Borchardt, it contains a shopping arcade, restaurants, a theatre as well as offices. In the tradition of the building's history, it has, once again, been extended by the addition of a five-star hotel. Unlike other additions to historic buildings where the architect is required to imitate an existing structure, this one is in stark contrast and is quite successful. The addition, a braced steel structure, is hung up and over the brick block. Steel panels and glass clad the struc-

Ganz + Rolfes/W R Borchardt/Kühn, Bergander, Bley

Ganz + Rolfes/W R Borchardt/Kühn, Bergander, Bley

ture and all metal parts are painted a deep turquoise. Without a doubt this is the most successful project in the Spreebogen complex due to its juxtaposition of the new and the old.

The most visible structure is the U-shaped office building known as 'Spreebogen', with its two rounded glazed towers facing the river's edge. Here, the architects Kühn, Bergander, Bley made no attempt to break down the development into separate articulated buildings, as is the case at Teleport and the old mill. As a result its simple shapes seem massive and overpowering, yet they are visually striking when seen at a distance.

The adjoining apartment building executed by the same architects is by contrast handled with much more care and agility. A conscious decision was taken to differentiate industrial and commercial functions from housing through the use of colour.

Taken as a whole, the complex is successful – not only for its developers but also for the adjoining area.

ADDRESS Alt Moabit (between Stromstraße and Kirchstraße), Berlin-Tiergarten [N–11]
ARCHITECTS W R Borchardt (old dairy building); Ganz + Rolfes (Teleport); Kühn, Bergander, Bley (Spreebogen)
U-BAHN Turmstraße
S-BAHN Bellevue
BUS 123, 245
ACCESS open

Ganz + Rolfes/W R Borchardt/Kühn, Bergander, Bley

Ganz + Rolfes/W R Borchardt/Kühn, Bergander, Bley

Housing, Huttenstraße

The district of Moabit was, and still is, dominated by large factories and their associated workers' housing. The general impression is one of heavy, massive and dark blocks. The most important piece of architecture in the area is the AEG turbine hall by Peter Behrens, one of the masterpieces of what is now labelled classic modernism.

The work of a less well-known master is the inspiration for this new building: the 1920s apartment blocks of Erwin Gutkind. Gutkind's trademark was his treatment and handling of the corner entrance; the play of brickwork and render; and an emphasis on the horizontal.

The architect, Klaus Meier-Hartmann, has reinterpreted these elements and used them in this work. The result is a building that has a clear relationship with the adjoining area and its history and that satisfies the requirements of today's social housing programme.

ADDRESS Huttenstraße 41, corner Wiebestraße, Berlin-Moabit [L–11]
U-BAHN Turmstraße
BUS 101, 123, 126, 227, 341
ACCESS open

Klaus Meier-Hartmann

Klaus Meier-Hartmann

Offices, Goslarer Ufer

Hidden in a little-known industrial area of Berlin, this building is located along a quiet canal. The E form of the building allows the green along the canal banks to be extended up into the courtyards. Along the Darwinstraße, a solid front is presented and maintained as it turns the corner. Through the differentiation of the lift towers as a separate element, the architectural expression of the front and side wing achieves an almost constructivist appearance.

The typical Berlin eaves line is maintained over the first five storeys. A 1.5-metre setback allows the upper two storeys to read as a separate roof element. The cladding of the lower storeys in natural stone and the roof in aluminium reinforces this reading.

At first, the size of this office building is quite overpowering. However, the more you study it, the more you discover. When viewed from the corner, it conjures up that famous image of Golosow from which the building's inspiration is drawn.

ADDRESS Goslarer Ufer, corner of Darwinstraße, Berlin-Charlottenburg [L–11]
CLIENT Quedlinburger Straße Grundstücksverwaltung GmbH
STRUCTURAL ENGINEER Hildebrandt & Sieber GmbH
COST DM 60 million
SIZE 25,200 square metres gross
U-BAHN Mierendorfplatz, Richard Wagner Platz
BUS 126, 127
ACCESS open

Moabit to Spandau

Steinebach & Weber 1992

Steinebach & Weber 1992

State Insurance Company headquarters

One of a series of incredibly large office complexes by Steinebach & Weber (see pages 24 and 38), this structure is actually a block within a block, complete with its own courtyard buildings.

The height of the long western façade is determined by the eaves lines of the housing blocks across the street. Vertical circulation towers play against the towers of these 1930s buildings and the upper floors step back to form terraces.

The seven-storey façade on Knobelsdorffstraße contains a five-storey glazed entrance hall, through which a glimpse of the interior courtyard is obtained. Along with its 'Casino' building housing the canteen and multipurpose rooms, this courtyard acts as a green lung for the high-density development.

A separate eight-storey tower is set off to the east, linked to the block with the customary glazed bridge. The tower and block use a reinforced-concrete, loadbearing skeleton system, clad in highly polished granite.

ADDRESS Knobelsdorffstraße 92, Berlin-Charlottenburg [J–10]
CLIENT LVA Landesversicherungsanstalt
STRUCTURAL ENGINEER Saar, Enseleit & Partner
COST DM 200 million
SIZE 62,000 square metres
U-BAHN Kaiserdamm
BUS 204
ACCESS none to courtyard

Moabit to Spandau

Steinebach & Weber 1995

Moabit to Spandau

Steinebach & Weber 1995

Youth centre

'Ecological building' is *the* current phrase. Some argue that it means no industrial products such as aluminum or PVC, others that it is to do with active and passive solar energy; to others still it means timber construction. American, Canadian, and even Bavarian carpenters are used to building entirely out of wood, but not the northern Germans. Here, masonry and concrete are the materials of choice while timber is perceived as cheap and non-durable. During this building's construction Austrian carpenters had to be called in to carry out the work.

The centre consists of two buildings, the larger one a two-storey south-facing structure containing an office and activity room tract, with a multi-purpose assembly room angled to the southwest to capture the late-afternoon sun. The smaller building has a relatively closed appearance since it contains changing rooms and showers for the adjacent sports fields.

The main challenge was the fire regulations. In Berlin both materials and their thickness are prescribed by the codes. In order to gain approval, it was necessary for the structural engineer to calculate in detail the tensions of the timber columns. As a result these tensions are directly reflected in their conical shape. This concept has led to some delicate and finely handled detailing. Unfortunately, it was not carried through to the interior which appears somewhat heavy and primitive. Even so, this building is a positive breakthrough for Berlin.

ADDRESS Heckerdamm 204–210, Berlin-Charlottenburg [K–12]
STRUCTURAL ENGINEER IFB Frohloff, Staffa, Thal, Kühn, Ecker
COST DM 5.4 million
U-BAHN Jakob-Kaiser-Platz
BUS 109,121,123
ACCESS afternoons

Moabit to Spandau

Klaus Meier-Hartmann 1996

Klaus Meier-Hartmann 1996

Spandauer Tor

The approach to Spandau from the east is marked to the right and left by the fine brick buildings of the Siemens Company. However, the last kilometre dissolves into a clutter of industrial and retail complexes scattered randomly like confetti. In order to give a focal point and identity to this area, Claude Vasconi proposed placing a large object in the middle of a mess (*á la* La Défense in Paris). Here, two 62-metre-high office towers were to flank the north and south edges of the main road to form a kind of gate (*Tor*). Behind them was planned a series of long office blocks, their height receding as they approached the river. All the blocks would be connected to their respective towers through a glass gallery, allowing them to be rented individually or *en masse*.

The market for rentable office space in Berlin has collapsed, so only one of these buildings has been completed; the second block, with its crane, remains uncompleted on the deserted building site. The completed building is of steel and glass, with a curved roof element. The glass walls are not perpendicular with the ground; instead, they tilt downwards and have external sun screens attached above. This combination reduces the extreme heatgain/loss normally associated with glazed structures. Though the façade and forms are dynamic and exciting, the hard facts of market forces are here to be seen.

ADDRESS Zitadellenweg 2–10, Berlin-Haselhorst [F–12]
CLIENT GbR Zitadellenweg und Zitadell GmbH
COST DM 300 million
SIZE 110,000 square metres
U-BAHN Zitadelle
BUS 153
ACCESS open

Claude Vasconi 1995

Claude Vasconi 1995

Tiergarten to Gatow

KITA, Lützowstraße

For this building – located in a block whose street edges, but not its interior – were destroyed by the war, the architects decided to develop the idea of fragmentation instead of recreating the street edge. Besides repairing the block edge where no interior buildings exist and turning the interior into green space, the other theory of the IBA (International Building Exhibition) was to repair the block interior where it did survive and to place social infrastructure and parks on the bombed-out edges along the street.

Thus freed from the implications of recreating the street edge, the architects placed the building according to purely functional needs. The 75 children who use the KITA (day-care centre) are divided into three mixed-age groups, each group having its own sleeping, eating and toilet areas. Stepped towards the south, sunlight penetrates into these rooms and on to the external terraces throughout the day.

The main assembly hall doubles as an all-weather play area and is located to the east, taking advantage of the morning sun. Similarly, the outdoor playground is located to the west for afternoon and after-school activities.

The materials chosen are warm and natural, in contrast to the primary colours normally associated with nursery schools. The atmosphere is friendly and relaxed, yet the architectural forms and spaces also make it an exciting environment.

The careful attention to detailing is the result of almost all the construction being carried out by building apprentices. The building gives a sense of being handcrafted, especially the wintergarden with its concentric yet decreasing quarter-circle vault beams.

Since completion, the metal-clad wall to the street has received its first graffiti. This actually adds to the building's rough but elegant appearance.

Tiergarten to Gatow

Halfmann und Zillich 1993

Halfmann und Zillich 1993

It is a building that fits perfectly into its fragmented site, thus verifying its urban-design concept. The centre is perfectly logical in its organisation, yet creative in its architectural response.

ADDRESS Lützowstraße 41–42, Berlin-Tiergarten [O–9]
STRUCTURAL ENGINEER Professor M Manleitner
LANDSCAPE ARCHITECT Josef Metzler
COST DM 5 million
SIZE 1164 square metres gross
U-BAHN Nollendorfplatz, Kürfurstenstraße
BUS 341, 129
ACCESS open

Halfmann und Zillich 1993

Housing, Lützowplatz

Located next door to the Bar am Lützowplatz by Jürgen Sawade with its highly refined modernist interior, this building is evidence as to why many consider Axel Schultes to be the finest architect in Berlin.

Owing to the shadows cast by the 60-metre-long fire wall next door, the courtyard was deemed to be undesirable as the focus of the flats. Instead the flats look on to the street front and are accessed from a single-loaded rear deck. The flats are conceived as maisonettes and the main façade reflects the proportions of the neighbouring buildings.

It is an elegant and refined composition. Its clarity is striking and the detailing is clean. The windows and their mullions are excellently proportioned and the entire building has been handled confidently.

ADDRESS Lützowplatz 5, Berlin-Tiergarten [O–9]
U-BAHN Wittenburgplatz, Nollendorfplatz
BUS 129, 341, 106
ACCESS open

Axel Schultes 1987

Axel Schultes 1987

Japanese-German Centre

The building was initially constructed between 1938 and 1942. After the war, it was left as a bomb-damaged ruin until 1986. The interiors of the main building have now been restored where possible to their original, impressive and overpowering condition.

The wing was totally replanned and the interior is now sleek and modern in appearance. Various additions to the back of the main building have been carried out, also in a very modern manner. A new Japanese garden was laid out to the rear, in stark contrast to the wild uncontrolled growth in the surrounding landscape of ruins.

In this building the new and the old have been meshed with extreme care and precision. It is an excellent example of the way a high standard of detailing and a clear design concept can achieve something that is greater than the sum of its parts.

ADDRESS Tiergartenstraße 24–27,
Berlin-Tiergarten [O–9]
CLIENT The Japanese-German Centre
Foundation, Berlin
COST DM 45 million
SIZE 8467 square metres gross
U-BAHN Kurfürstenstraße
BUS 129
ACCESS restricted

Kisho Kurokawa and Taiji Yamaguchi 1988

Salamanderhaus

Since the end of the Second World War, the uncertain political situation has discouraged speculators and corporations from building medium or large office blocks in Berlin. At one point, Berlin was ranked only thirteenth among German cities in terms of its desirability. Overnight that changed. The 1950s buildings with only one and two storeys along the main shopping streets of the Ku'damm and Tauentzien became valuable properties. Salamander decided to tear down their one-storey shoe shop and replace it with a modern, representative, mixed-use building.

The architects have responded with a very successful solution to the corner site and the art of shopping. At ground level, an arcade protects shoppers from the elements and invites customers in towards the large display windows and then into the store itself.

The arcade continues above the shop and through the upper levels in the form of a wintergarden between the exterior façade and the offices. Luxury flats are located in the set-back sixth floor and all levels are connected by a glass lift. The wintergarden is especially striking at night when the whole building becomes transparent from the street.

The architects have succeeded in setting a new standard for mixed-use accommodation in Berlin. This building does not shout, nor does it have to; its simple elegance speaks for itself.

ADDRESS Tauentzien 15, Berlin-Wilmersdorf [N–9]
CLIENT Salamander AG
COST DM 38 million
SIZE 8648 square metres usable space
U-BAHN Wittenbergplatz, Kurfürstendamm
BUS 119, 129, 146, 219
ACCESS open

von Gerkan, Marg und Partner 1992

von Gerkan, Marg und Partner 1992

Peek und Cloppenburg

As with the Salamanderhaus (see page 56), it was the economic pressures released after the fall of the Berlin Wall that supplied the impetus to demolish what was previously a two-storey clothing store. In order to maximise the value of the site, a structure encompassing the maximum, allowable building volume was erected.

The concept of the façade is clear and straightforward: a structural grid of precast concrete from which transparent 'curtains' are hung. These curtains do not simply hang vertically, but give the appearance of fluttering outwards, as if from an open window. They provide a canopy for passersby, but woe to those not walking directly underneath them when it rains!

The fire walls to the side and rear of the building have been covered with metal panels, awaiting the construction of their future neighbours.

Tiergarten to Gatow

ADDRESS corner of Tauentzien/Nürnberger Straße,
Berlin-Wilmersdorf [N–9]
CLIENT Peek und Cloppenburg KG
U-BAHN Wittenbergplatz
BUS 119, 129, 219, 146
ACCESS open during shopping hours

Gottfried and Peter Böhm 1995

Gottfried and Peter Böhm 1995

Löbbecke Bank

The basis of this composition is the historic Villa Ilse. The exterior has been restored and the interior has been converted into a banking centre. A glazed addition to the rear is connected to the villa by a flowing glass and steel bridge supported by a pylon.

The new office accommodation has two faces – glass and steel towards the villa and stone towards the Fasanenstraße – divided from each other by vertical circulation towers. The south façade reflects the height of the buildings across the street and the set-back roof floors tie in the neighbour to the south with the new glass and steel offices in the courtyard.

This is a fine and exciting piece of urban design, combining the historical with the new. The architecture is also well integrated into its setting; it manages to respect its context while being bold in its expression.

Tiergarten to Gatow

ADDRESS Fasanenstraße 75/76, Berlin-Charlottenburg [M–9]
CLIENT Löbbecke Bank
COST DM 75 million
S-BAHN Uhlandstraße
BUS 109, 119, 129
ACCESS open

W R Borchardt 1994

W R Borchardt 1994

Kant-Dreieck

Already a fixture on the Berlin skyline, this recently completed building is the subject of intense debate. Much has been made of the difficulties of the site. Though it is not unlike other normal street corners, at the back the railroad arches curve into the site, slicing it into a triangle. The architect solved the problems thrown up by the oddly shaped plot in an extremely refined way, as if it were the only possible, rational solution. An office tower has been placed squarely at the corner and a lower building, which respects the height of its neighbours' eaves, attaches itself to it.

By proposing a tower, the architect has been able to achieve an economically viable density ratio while giving over necessary public space to the street. This creates a massing which is relaxed and appropriate to the area.

The lower building is undoubtedly the better of the two: a slick, clean, elegant, thoroughly modern office block. The tower is in fact a column with base, shaft and capital. Unfortunately, due to height restrictions, the column appears as two stacked cubes with a sail on top.

Aside from the tower, it is the sail that catches the eye. Actually a solar-heat collector, this 34-tonne, riveted, sheet-metal weather vane turns according to the sun's orientation, giving the ensemble an ever-changing composition. Already visitors are asking: 'Where's the building with the vane?' Unfortunately, commercialism and bad taste have overtaken events and the vane now doubles as an advertising billboard.

A small sex shop and its neighbouring building to the east of the complex – relics of postwar Berlin – currently stand in the way of completing the landscaping. Their juxtaposition to Kant-Dreieck and to the theatre across the street presents to the viewer a Berlin that will soon disappear, a Berlin of opposites, of contrasts, of the unexpected.

Professor Josef P Kleihues 1994

Professor Josef P Kleihues 1994

With this project, Berlin is healing at long last a visible wound. Kant-Dreieck, for all the controversy it has raised, is a building that will eventually grow on Berliners.

ADDRESS Kantstraße 155, Berlin-Charlottenburg [M–9]
U-BAHN Zoologischer Garten, Savigny Platz
S-BAHN Zoologischer Garten, Savigny Platz
BUS 149
ACCESS open

Professor Josef P Kleihues 1994

Professor Josef P Kleihues 1994

Berlin Stock Exchange

Nicholas Grimshaw's new stock exchange and communication centre is bound to become a topic of discussion within Berlin architectural circles.

The main bulk of the building, containing offices for a variety of organisations, respects the traditional eaves height of the surrounding buildings. A central spine runs down the middle of the site, acting as an internal street which will be open to the public, allowing views into the trading floor itself as well as into the exhibition spaces. The most unusual feature of the building came about as a result of the client's requirement for an unobstructed ground-floor plan. The upper storeys are suspended from a series of 15 in-situ concrete arches which span from the front of the building to the back. The differing arch sizes result from the irregular site boundary. Two large atriums are located within the complex, allowing for natural daylight and ventilation.

The aesthetics of the exchange will be hotly debated upon completion. Many excellent buildings have recently been completed by local architects, but Berlin will only finally lose its provinciality through the work of international designers such as Nicholas Grimshaw, Richard Rogers, Renzo Piano and Jean Nouvel.

ADDRESS Fasanenstraße, Berlin-Charlottenburg [M–9]
CLIENT IHM, VBKI
STRUCTURAL ENGINEER Whitby & Bird
COST DM 150 million
SIZE 38,000 square metres gross
U-BAHN Ernst Reuter Platz, Bahnhof Zoo
S-BAHN Bahnhof Zoo, Savigny Platz
BUS 145, 149, 245
ACCESS open

Nicholas Grimshaw & Partners 1995

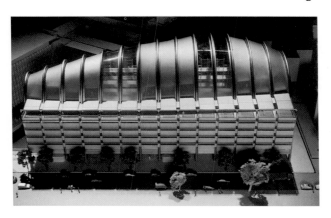

Nicholas Grimshaw & Partners 1995

Offices, Ku'damm 70

Berlin meets Chicago, whether it likes it or not. Here is clearly demonstrated Berlin's provinciality. A different class of architecture has arrived but it's in the wrong place! The Ku'damm is not South Wacker Drive. The building is too tall and the 'constructivist spire' is laughable. The materials, though, are sleek, the mullions exquisite, the breaking up of the glass expanse brilliantly conceived and executed.

The fact that this building is so narrow (2.9 metres on the ground floor and 5.5 metres at the highest level) is to its advantage; it becomes small and almost jewel-like. With an innovative spire, the architects could conceivably have pulled it off.

Although this is a building of great quality and skill, Zaha Hadid's design for this site should have been built instead.

ADDRESS Kurfürstendamm 70, Berlin-Charlottenburg [L–9]
CLIENT EUWO Bauträger
STRUCTURAL ENGINEER BFM Friedrich Müller
COST DM 24 million
SIZE 1200 square metres net
U-BAHN Adenauer Platz
BUS 109, 119, 129, 219
ACCESS open

Tiergarten to Gatow

Murphy/Jahn 1994

Housing, Konstanzer Straße

The buildings destroyed here were not reconstructed after the war as they became subject to 1950s urban-planning theory. The southeast-facing corner was left open to let sunlight penetrate the block's inner courtyard. A small car park and a few trees highlighted the unsatisfactory urban situation. Now the immense pressure to build affordable housing in the city centre has led to a rethink of this typical Berlin corner, and the architect has responded in an appropriate way.

The building attaches itself to its turn-of-the-century neighbour, but does not follow the street edge to the corner. Instead, it becomes a tower, compensating for the density lost by not building out to the corner. It almost touches its 1950s neighbour, but leaves a gap as large wide enough for passage into the revitalised courtyard. A brick wall with steel railings wraps around the corner, acting as a screen for the green space directly in front of the ground-floor balcony of the adjacent building. On the east face, several flats have bay windows angled slightly away from the Konstanzer Straße, again providing some privacy. The courtyard is now a green lung for the buildings fronting the street and those lying deep in the block. Play areas have been provided. The 1950s block has been repainted; from the corner it could almost be mistaken for a new composition. This is the success of the building: it corrects its context, raising the quality of the surrounding buildings and the street.

ADDRESS Konstanzer Straße 7, Düsseldorfer Straße 31A,
Berlin-Wilmersdorf [L–8]
STRUCTURAL ENGINEER Reimer + Partner
U-BAHN Konstanzer Straße
BUS 101
ACCESS open

Sabine Klose 1992

Sabine Klose 1992

Offices, Ku'damm 119

This new office block actually sits on the axis at the end of Berlin's most prestigious street: the Kurfürstendamm. At this point the boulevard swings to the left and terminates at a traffic roundabout.

Murphy/Jahn's building curves to deflect the traffic to the left as well as to turn the corner to the side street. It has a simple steel and glass façade, but the whole is 'crowned' with a steel-roof element that shades the set-back upper storey.

The building steps down to the corners, eventually matching the height of its neighbours. Technically, it responds well to its urban situation, but without drama.

Of more interest are the two concrete Cadillacs by Wolf Vostell which make a definitive statement on the current urban situation.

ADDRESS Kurfürstendamm 119,
Berlin-Wilmersdorf [K–8]
CLIENT Athena Grundstücks AG
COST DM 70 million
SIZE 15,000 square metres gross
S-BAHN Hallensee
BUS 110, 119, 129
ACCESS open

Murphy/Jahn 1995

Offices, Halensee Straße

The challenges facing the architects of this dynamic project were enormous, but the dictates of site, programme and technical system requirements have been used to positive effect. The left-over site, wedged between existing housing blocks and the autobahn, caused major problems in optimising rentable area. A base was constructed to house the required parking garage and pocket park which are also used by the neighbouring blocks. The main office space is housed in a lemon-wedge-shaped tower, which in part cantilevers up to 6 metres over the autobahn. The shape and positioning of the wedge towards the sharp end of the site preserve the views and sunlight exposure of its neighbours.

The second problem was the noise and smog pollution of the autobahn itself. As an economical solution to the resulting M+ E requirements, a double-skinned façade facing the motorway was proposed. The exterior skin is fixed single-pane glazing, the interior skin is thermal insulated glass in the form of sliding panels. The 85-centimetre gap between them acts as sound insulation as well as a passive collector of solar energy. To control overheating, sun shades are installed on the interior face of the exterior glazing, and small pipes protruding through the exterior glazing allow excess heat to escape and double as smoke outlets in case of fire. The sliding panels allow the users access to this space and a limited control of their working environment.

ADDRESS Bornimer Straße, Halensee Straße [K–8]
CLIENT Mübau, Berlin
ENGINEER IBS Ing.-Büro Schalm (façade)
S-BAHN Halensee
BUS 110, 119
ACCESS open

Tiergarten to Gatow

Léon + Wohlhage 1996

Léon + Wohlhage 1996

Messe extension

This is the scale at which O M Ungers works best. The programme called for an additional 60,000 square metres to be added to an already immense exhibition complex. Another requirement was bringing order to the complex as a whole; currently the exhibition grounds are a chaotic collection of nondescript sheds which have been added piecemeal over the years to the original, stone-clad structures.

Ungers' solution is quite straightforward: a thin long tract attaches itself to the existing main building, respecting its height and width. From this new structure, three larger exhibition halls are attached at right angles, forming the fourth side of the courtyard garden and forming an edge to the street.

The treatment of the façade is similarly at a larger-than life scale, with Ungers' trademark squares dominating.

Tiergarten to Gatow

ADDRESS Messedamm, Berlin-Charlottenburg [J–9]
CLIENT Land Berlin
SIZE 64,000 square metres (extension)
U-BAHN Theodor-Heuss-Platz
S-BAHN Halensee
BUS 219, 149, 104
ACCESS on exhibition dates only

Professor O M Ungers 1997

Professor O M Ungers 1997

Heinz-Galinski school

This is the first elementary school purpose-built for Jewish and non-Jewish children since the war. Berlin's Jewish community has doubled since the collapse of the Soviet Union. However, many of the newcomers do not have a strong sense of Jewish culture. This school is intended to educate the young and their parents about the fun side of Jewish life – music, literature and dance – and to show the non-Jewish community that Jewish culture in Berlin did not end with the Holocaust.

The international competition held in 1990 for the school's design was won by the Israeli architect Zvi Hecker. The concept derives from a sunflower, the plant on which the architect survived while escaping his native Poland during the war. From this starting point, the design begins to spin like a centrifuge, the individual building parts flaring out from the centre. This leads to the further distortion of the forms that make up the building programme, so that in the end no two rooms are identical. Credit must also be given to the contact architect Inken Baller for giving the idea concrete form and solving the endless detailing problems.

Whether deconstructivist or organic, this building is a welcome departure from the so-called official Berlin style of punched holes in stone-clad façades which is currently being sold as great architecture. One only needs to look at the work of Hans Scharoun to realise that Berlin has not one but several architectural traditions.

ADDRESS Waldschulallee, Berlin-Charlottenburg [H–9]
CLIENT Jüdische Gemeinde zu Berlin
COST DM 46.3 million
S-BAHN Halensee
BUS 219
ACCESS by appointment only

Zvi Hecker 1995

Horst-Korber Sports Centre

Less than 200 metres from the 1936 Olympic Stadium complex, the new indoor sports centre is a beautiful addition to the area's facilities. The building programme called not only for a multipurpose hall, but also for the facilities needed to condition athletes for peak performance: weight rooms, saunas, whirlpools, a cafeteria, rooms for courses and seminars, even an athletes' hotel. It is a world unto itself, set into the landscape. The main hall is sunk into the natural slope of the terrain, its only visible element being a curved roof with 420 rooflights which provide a regular, nondazzling natural light for the hall below.

The hotel and cafeteria are located to the north, their two storeys rising above the natural slope. The gap between these two buildings and the hall serves as the main entrance for both. Located under the gap are the changing rooms. Thus, the two buildings are linked by the sequential progression of the athletes themselves – the paths of the public and the participants never cross.

The structural and material composition of the complex is as well carried out as the programme's organisation. Eight 30-metre-high pylons resembling trees carry cables anchored into the ground and attached to the roof of the main hall, enabling the depth of the roof trusses to be reduced to a minimum. Lightweight textured steel plates are hung from the entrance façade of the cafeteria, giving a shimmering red-violet reflection when hit by sunlight. Opposite this, full-height glass doors and windows dominate the spectators' entrances. Concrete surfaces and stairs are treated in new and creative ways. Even fire doors are turned into exciting visual elements. The more one looks, the more one discovers.

The interior of the main hall is thought out with just as much care. The treatment of the folding-out tribune and the walls is so simple that

Christoph Langhof, Thomas Hänni, Herbert Meerstein 1990

Christoph Langhof, Thomas Hänni, Herbert Meerstein 1990

you wonder why it has not been done before. The quality of light, and of the space itself, is exquisite.

Here, sports-architecture has been elevated to a higher plane. Here, sport is treated as culture, as valuable as opera, art and education.

ADDRESS Glockenturmstraße,
Berlin-Charlottenburg [F–10]
CLIENT Landessportbund Berlin eV
SIZE 15,800 square metres
U-BAHN Olympia-Stadion
BUS 218, 149
ACCESS open

Christoph Langhof, Thomas Hänni, Herbert Meerstein 1990

Christoph Langhof, Thomas Hänni, Herbert Meerstein 1990

Sports hall at Windmühlenberg

Driving to Gatow, you wonder if you're still in Berlin or out in the country. The idyllic landscape of lakes, forests and meadows is extremely impressive and beautiful. Hidden behind trees, the reality of divided Berlin can be seen: the British military airport. However, planes no longer disturb the tranquility of this place.

The building on Am Kinderdorf, built as a hospital in the late 1930s, was soon converted into a school. For its first 60 years it lacked an indoor sports facility, but this has now been added. Behind the main building to the right, a small, sensitive incision has been made into the landscape. A simple curve has been sliced out of the earth to provide access to the underground facilities. To the left, a grass-covered roof hides changing rooms and facilities for the playing fields above. To the right, behind a rich brick retaining-wall screen, are the facilities for the adjacent gym. Owing to the height requirements of volley ball, a lightweight steel roof structure pops up out of the ground, supported by steel v-braces.

Glass windows wrap around all four sides, providing a transparent visual effect. Sun shades incorporated into the underside of the roof structure are automatically lowered as the sun moves around the building. The windows, which are openable, are controlled by a wind vane and are self-closing when high wind speeds occur.

This is no bunker. The hall is a beautiful element sitting comfortably in the landscape.

ADDRESS Am Kinderdorf, Berlin-Gatow [D–8]
CLIENT Bezirksamt Spandau
STRUCTURAL ENGINEER Professor Dr Ing. Franz Josef Hilbers
BUS 134, 334
ACCESS open

Tiergarten to Gatow

Benedict Tonon 1993

Benedict Tonon 1993

Schöneberg to Steglitz

Galeria department store

The main concept is transparency, making everything on the inside apparent to those on the outside. As with any department store, the goods are displayed in the ground-floor windows. Here, the entire store is on display, as well as the customers inside. Escalators are located near the façade so as to be seen from the main shopping street. A glass lift is located near the entrance door. Through the dynamic movement of people and machinery, the hustle and bustle of street life is continued inside and revealed to the outside.

Galeria is a departure from the larger Berlin department stores with their decorated-shed walls containing little or no fenestration. This building, although small, has already had a major impact on retail design in Berlin.

ADDRESS Schloßstraße, Berlin-Steglitz [M–5]
CLIENT Ingeborg and Peter Fritz
STRUCTURAL ENGINEER H J Weinhol/Technisches Büro Fa. Ing. Bau GmbH
COST DM 16 million
SIZE 5150 square metres
U-BAHN Schloßstraße
BUS 148, 186, 383
ACCESS shopping hours

Quick-Bäckmann-Quick 1995

Quick-Bäckmann-Quick 1995

B1 House 40

This is an urban-design success from which Berlin can learn. Until the 1990s the site was a fragmented area, damaged first by the war and then, more seriously, by urban planning theories and practices. What was left was a 22-metre-high *Brandwand* (fire wall) to the west, a ruined villa to the north, a few trees sprinkled about and a 1950s glass pavilion (now listed) used as a car showroom.

The response of the architects was to provide a transition from the typical *Blockrandbebauung* (street-edge building) to the freestanding villa by turning the street façade around the corner to the platz through the use of an ever-so-slightly curved reinforced-concrete façade element. As it approaches the villa, the ratio of glass to solid increases, reflecting the trees and thereby softening the effect of the building's mass.

The architects have succeeded in transforming a fragmented corner into a real urban place. The vw pavilion has become the focal point of the platz, but now the restored villa with its decorative façade has the opportunity to show itself off to the public.

ADDRESS Schloßstraße 40, Berlin-Steglitz [M–5]
CLIENT Haberent Grundstücks GmbH Berlin
STRUCTURAL ENGINEER Polonyi und Fink
COST DM 11 million
SIZE 3800 square metres gross
U-BAHN Rathaus Steglitz U-9
BUS 148, 183, 186
ACCESS open

Assmann Salomon und Scheidt 1992

Assmann Salomon und Scheidt 1992

Housing, Bürgipfad

Leftover or undeveloped sites next to the Berlin Wall were relatively worthless before 1990; they were considered to be at the end of the world. The fact that your view from the living room would be blocked by a 3-metre-high wall was not considered a selling point.

With the fall of the Wall, the value of these properties rocketed. The former death strip suddenly became a valuable asset as a linear park, just on your doorstep.

The architects have used the orientation of the site to their advantage; the main access to the complex is from the north, as are the entrances to the individual units. Living rooms and gardens are all oriented to the south. The units themselves are a mixture of small apartments, maisonettes and terraced houses. There are two basic house types, with only the colour of the timber cladding marking them out individually.

The buildings and the site planning drew their inspiration from 1920s modernism. They also owe a debt to the *Neue Sachlichkeit* thinking of the 1980s, but have through their detailing a clear 1990s identity. Eventually, this development will be overgrown with plants and trees – a green Weissenhof for the turn of the century.

ADDRESS Bürgipfad 22–24, Berlin-Steglitz [M-1]
S-BAHN Lichterfelde-Ost
BUS 180, 277, 280
ACCESS open

Wiechers + Beck

Wiechers + Beck

Kreuzberg to Neukölln

SPD headquarters

Situated on a triangular site, this office building helps to repair the historical urban fabric of Kreuzberg. Taking its inspiration from Erich Mendelsohn's IG Metall headquarters, the main entrance addresses the corner, with two office wings radiating out to the north from this point. The building, despite being the headquarters of one of Germany's largest political parties, is conceived as being open and accessible to the public. Shops along the street frontage, a passage connecting Wilhelmstraße and Stresemannstraße, an atrium that serves as a public gathering and exhibition space, and a public cafeteria above the entrance, all attempt to bring the residents of the area into contact with the politicians.

The exterior respects the traditional 22-metre eaves height of Kreuzberg, only breaking it to emphasise the corner entrance. The extensive use of glass is a literal attempt to translate the party's ideas of transparency and democracy into architectural form.

This ambitious attempt to integrate the public and politicians is a welcome addition to Kreuzberg. Its location in the most left-wing/green political area of former West Berlin is itself a political statement. However, the gentrification of Kreuzberg has begun, and the Social Democrats may soon find themselves surrounded by unsympathetic neighbours.

ADDRESS Wilhelmstraße and Stresemannstraße, Berlin-Kreuzberg [Q–9]
CLIENT SPD
STRUCTURAL ENGINEER Professor Polonyi and Professor Bollinger
COST DM 90 million
SIZE 21,000 square metres of useable space
U-BAHN Hallesches Tor
BUS 341
ACCESS open

Kreuzberg to Neukölln

Professor Helge Bofinger + Partner 1995

Kreuzberg to Neukölln

Professor Helge Bofinger + Partner 1995

The Jewish Museum

In 1988, after a quarter century of debate, it was decided to hold an architectural competition for the building of an extension to the Berlin Museum, documenting the history of the Jewish community in the city. Daniel Libeskind was awarded first prize for his outstanding entry.

Libeskind's proposal was based on three ideas:

First, the impossibility of understanding the history of Berlin without understanding the enormous intellectual, economic and cultural contribution made by the Jewish citizens of Berlin. Second, the necessity to integrate physically and spiritually the meaning of the Holocaust into the consciousness and memory of the city of Berlin. Third, that only through the acknowledgement and incorporation of this absence and void of Jewish life in Berlin can the history of Berlin and Europe have a future.

The museum is organised around three criss-crossing axes. The first leads, eventually, to a dead end: the Holocaust Museum. The second leads to the exterior garden, representing the exile and emigration of Jews around the world. The third leads to the exhibition floor of the Berlin and Jewish Museums.

Intersecting all three is a central axis consisting of a void. Bridges linking various parts of the museum traverse the void. Its walls are covered with the names of Jewish citizens of Berlin who were deported and exterminated. As visitors walk through the museum, they will experience the void left by those whose names they can read.

The symbolism of the museum's programme overpowers any description of the construction techniques employed. The reinforced-concrete walls with their unique shaped openings were erected, creating a land-

Daniel Libeskind 1999

Kreuzberg to Neukölln

Daniel Libeskind 1999

scape of freestanding sculptural objects during the construction phase.

The new building is connected to the existing Berlin Museum underground, thus preserving the individual personalities of the two institutions. The façades in no way relate to each other, but the programme unites them, creating an experience that is more than bricks and mortar.

In Libeskind's words, the building 'is organised around a centre which is not, around what is not visible. And what is not visible is the richness of the former Jewish heritage in Berlin, since physically it has disappeared'.

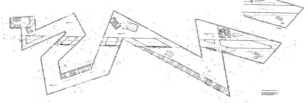

ADDRESS Lindenstraße 15, Berlin-Kreuzeberg [Q–9]
CLIENT Land Berlin
STRUCTURAL ENGINEER GSE Saar, Enseleit and Partner;
IGW Ingenieurgruppe Wiese
COST DM 115 million
SIZE 12,000 square metres net
U-BAHN Hallesches Tor, Kochstraße
BUS 141
ACCESS under construction

Daniel Libeskind 1999

Daniel Libeskind 1999

TAZ building

Without doubt this is the finest piece of architecture to be built in Berlin within the last ten years.

The adjoining listed 1906 building (Kochstraße 18) is itself a great work. With its classical elements and decoration offset by the thoroughly modern 1920s-style, curved, glazed bay windows (clearly ahead of their time), it sits quietly and confidently amid the chaos of the traffic-ridden Kochstraße.

The TAZ newspaper decided to relocate its headquarters back to this prewar publishing area (Mendelsohn's newly reconstructed Mosse publishing headquarters is two blocks away; see page 154), but needed approximately double the existing floor area. Thus the twin building was born, but not an identical one. In no way, shape or form has the architect played with historical pastiche.

This building is modern through and through. Its use of proportions is what makes it outstanding. The architect has used the same floor-to-floor heights as the existing building, and the balconies and their railings also have similar proportions to the windows of the older structure, allowing them to act as a screen and tie the two together. The roof storey is set back from the edge, thus respecting the eaves height of its neighbour.

The balconies fly out and around to help turn the corner to the 'park'. The green space is left over from an abandoned road-widening scheme but will remain because of a nearby old people's home.

The extensive use of glass allows light to penetrate deep into the interior, as in number 18. A common stair and lift serve both buildings and a second means of emergency escape is incorporated into the rear of the new structure. A wide-span, steel-beam construction has been used to create a completely column-free interior to allow for maximum flexibility of office arrangement.

Gerhard Spangenberg 1991

Kreuzberg to Neukölln

Gerhard Spangenberg 1991

The architect has managed to fulfil the client's brief, to complement without imitating its neighbour, and to create a delight for the eye. You only need to stand across the street and study the buildings to see how similar and yet how different they are. You are looking at modernism handled with conviction.

ADDRESS Kochstraße 19, Berlin-Kreuzberg [Q–9]
CLIENT Die Tageszeitung
U-BAHN Kochstraße
BUS 129
ACCESS open

Gerhard Spangenberg 1991

Gerhard Spangenberg 1991

Sale e Tabacchi

The transition of Kreuzberg is exemplified by the presence of this bar/restaurant, for even three years ago such an establishment would have been unthinkable in this location.

Formerly, this area was war-shattered and broken, with only the remaining street patterns giving hints of a former urbanism. During the 1980s, the IBA (International Building Exhibition) tried to inject new life into this part of the city through the building of social housing and schools, but it was still difficult to attract businesses and jobs. After the collapse of the Berlin Wall and the subsequent spurt in office space construction along the former death strip, a different type of infrastructure was seen to be needed here, that of an urban watering hole for the upper classes, a place to drink, eat well, and to socialise at lunch and after work.

The name and interior design of this restaurant evoke a time when the sale of salt and tobacco was monopolised by the state and could only be obtained in public bars, hence the two sales counters to the left as one enters. The central space is long and narrow, reinforced by the bar and the bench seating. The main dining room is at the rear with a garden opening off it.

The use of colour is refined, the detailing well thought out and executed with a high level of craftsmanship. It is a delightful and relaxing oasis on this chaotic street.

ADDRESS Kochstraße 18, Berlin-Kreuzberg [Q–9]
U-BAHN Kochstraße
BUS 142, 147, 129
ACCESS open

Max Dudler 1996

Max Dudler 1996

Housing, Oranienstraße

The starting point for this building was its need to integrate with the adjacent 1960s housing estate. The existing blocks of flats are oriented to the south and west, with slight regard to the street edges. Through careful positioning and the adoption of the same slant to the street edge as the existing buildings, the architects have re-established the line along Oranienstraße, tying the old in with the new.

The architects have sliced their building programmatically in two: kitchens, baths and circulation are towards the busy street front; living and sleeping accommodation is towards the quieter and sunny rear. These two slices are then shifted in relation to each other, enabling the architects to choose different materials for the façades. The rich brickwork of the front picks up the trim around the entrances of the 1960s blocks and acts as a transition to the massive, 1920s brick office building on the opposite corner, while the render on the back relates to the bulk of the 1960s apartments.

In keeping with Berlin tradition, there are shops on the ground floor. The floor area they require creates large terraces for the first-floor flats.

The entire building is an exercise in sensitive urban design. The requirements of the site and scheme are quietly integrated into each other, resulting in a building that does not need to shout for attention in order to be recognised for its quality. The architects' penchant for modesty and understatement also means that their work does not often appear in the international architectural press.

ADDRESS Oranienstraße 110, Berlin-Kreuzberg [Q–9]
U-BAHN Kochstraße
BUS 129, 141
ACCESS open

Maedebach, Redeleit + Partners 1995

Maedebach, Redeleit + Partners 1995

Görlitzer Bahnhof swimming complex

The former Görlitzer Bahnhof once occupied this site. After the war it was left as a ruin in a derelict landscape. It was only in 1978 that the decision was taken to create an inner-city park for this densely populated area. Small outbuildings of the station were preserved along with the rubble near the western edge. Various sports facilities, including special areas for rollerskating and skateboarding, are provided. The mountain of rubble is taken over by mountainbikers during the summer and kids' sledges during the winter.

Integrated with the rubble is a remarkable piece of urban infrastructure – an indoor swimming complex. In contrast to Blub, a middle-class leisure centre in Berlin, this facility reaches out to the unemployed, the disabled, the low paid and to the large Turkish community of the area.

The building is divided into three parts. On the platz is a two-storey rendered structure which houses the entrance, changing rooms, showers and the cafeteria. Its limited fenestration reflects the need for privacy as dictated by its functions. Proceeding from the changing rooms, you enter the second structure containing the main swimming hall with several types of pool all under one structurally unique roof. The construction defies description; it has to be seen to be believed. The sides of the hall are fully glazed and the roof is perforated with numerous skylights providing natural daylight and ventilation. Continuing on, you enter the third structure, containing a diving pool and saunas. This is actually built into the rubble and disappears into it when viewed from the street. One pool manages to push itself through the hill, poking out again on the other side with its glazed exterior wall.

According to the staff, there is only one problem with the pedestrian circulation within the complex, but this is easily overcome by cleaning the floors of the staircase more often.

Christoph Langhof, Thomas Hänni, Herbert Meerstein 1987

Kreuzberg to Neukölln

Christoph Langhof, Thomas Hänni, Herbert Meerstein 1987

In all, this building and its site are unique and both are perfectly designed for the neighbourhood and its residents. The roof construction over the main pools is quite striking at night. The architect deserves high praise for his unique contribution to Berlin's architecture.

ADDRESS Spreewaldplatz, Berlin-Kreuzberg [T–8]
CLIENT Bezirksamt Kreuzberg
STRUCTURAL ENGINEER Professor M Manleitner, Herbert Schutsch
U-BAHN Görlitzer Bahnhoff
BUS 129
ACCESS open

Christoph Langhof, Thomas Hänni, Herbert Meerstein 1987

Housing, Schlesische Straße

This block, located in a densely populated area of Berlin, was heavily damaged during the war. It was further destroyed by 1960s planning theories which failed to respect the old street line. The architects, seeing no way to correct the situation, decided to use these mistakes to their advantage.

The building sits as an independent object on the corner, neither acknowledging nor tying in with its neighbourhood. In order to compensate for the open space it gives to the block, the building is taller than normal with two roof storeys located above the 22-metre parapet line of the main floors. Towards the courtyard, a cascade of glass wintergardens is to be found, arranged in a zigzag, turning the interior corner.

The rooms of each flat are arranged without any hierarchy and are interconnected with sliding doors, allowing inhabitants to arrange their flats to suit their own particular lifestyle.

The development represents a very sensible solution to an ongoing urban problem in Berlin.

ADDRESS Schlesische Straße 22, Berlin-Kreuzberg [T–8]
CLIENT Batiment Gesellschaft für schlüsselfertiges Bauen
STRUCTURAL ENGINEER Professor Gerhard Pichler
COST DM 10 million
SIZE 3719 square metres gross
U-BAHN Schlesisches Tor
BUS 265
ACCESS open

Hilde Léon and Konrad Wohlhage 1994

Hilde Léon and Konrad Wohlhage 1994

Police headquarters

The exterior of this office block along the Tempelhofer Damm is on the same scale as the megalomania of the Nazis' built airport, the Flughafen Tempelhof, across the street. Long, almost endless, it conveys an omnipotence that perfectly expresses its function.

However, the interior courtyards are definitely its saving grace. Planted roofscapes and terraces step down towards a large artificial pond and a glass pavilion containing the canteen. A green oasis within and between a labyrinth of offices is the result, helping to make life bearable for the members of the police administration who work here every day.

ADDRESS Tempelhofer Damm, Kaiserkorso, Berlin-Tempelhof [P–7]
CLIENT Senatsverwaltung für Bau- und Wohnungswesen
STRUCTURAL ENGINEER Gauff-Ingenieure and Professor Polonyi
COST DM 350 million
SIZE 26,000 square metres net
U-BAHN Platz der Luftbrücke
BUS 104, 184
ACCESS open

Betz und Partner 1994

Betz und Partner 1994

Business centre Ullsteinhaus

The listed Ullsteinhaus, designed by Eugen Schmohl, is an outstanding example of 1920s state-of-the-art engineering. It is a reinforced-steel, skeleton-frame construction resting on replacement-type foundation piles. A printing works, it was designed around American theories of the rationalisation of transportation, circulation and organisation.

In addition, various artists, including Joseph Albers, Fritz Klimsch, Joseph Thorak and Wilhelm Gerstel, were commissioned to, in the words of the owner, 'give visitors an impression that reflects the significance of the company'. In today's terms they were employed to create a corporate identity.

The same theories were apparent 70 years later among a new generation of architects carrying out this extension. A three-storey industrial shed was erected towards the harbour side, its eaves lines adhering to those of the older extension along the canal. Towards the street, three office blocks were placed. Their slightly curved street façades differ from their red-dyed, artificial-stone sides: a grid of photovoltaic elements is mounted on them, producing enough power to light all the corridors in the complex. A three-storey base containing the main east–west circulation unites all three blocks.

Three independent vertical circulation towers intersect the buildings and, through their strategic placement, have eliminated the need for the traditional second means of escape, achieving a very high and profitable ratio of usable floor space to circulation area. The materials, which range from traditional brickwork to modern corrugated sheet metal, are skilfully handled. The detailing is surprisingly fine considering the scale of the project.

The complex is not only functional in terms of its programme, layout and state-of-the-art technology; it also incorporates artistic flair in the

Nalbach und Nalbach 1994

way the elements themselves – form, shape and colour – are handled. The building embodies quality and good design.

One of the most difficult and challenging briefs an architect can have is to build an extension to an existing architectural masterpiece. Here, the architects have succeeded.

ADDRESS Ullsteinstraße 136–142, Berlin-Tempelhof [Q–5]
CLIENT Becker and Kries
STRUCTURAL ENGINEER Fink GmbH
COST DM 250 million
SIZE 90 square metres
U-BAHN Ullsteinhaus
BUS 270
ACCESS open

Nalbach und Nalbach 1994

Nalbach und Nalbach 1994

Albert Einstein school extension

At first glance this extension is nothing spectacular. It is only when you start to study the existing school buildings and the urban situation that the apparent simplicity of the solution becomes devastatingly clear.

The 1950s school buildings were freestanding parallel pavilions, linked by a glass corridor. The brief called for an extension that would add more space and be equally accessible from the three easternmost buildings. An addition along the south was ruled out due to the limited courtyard space. Instead, the architect chose to place the building along the street edge, with the rooms arranged along a single-loaded corridor which connects all three existing buildings.

The elliptical form has the advantage of acting as a soft edge to the adjoining park, as well as leading visitors along to the entrance and then turning them towards the doors. The use of the ellipse prevents the repetitive brick façade from becoming boring as it is never seen in its entirety at any one point. The rear façade is carried out in white render, to tie in with the old school buildings. The new interior corridor linking the four buildings is naturally lit on all levels through the use of extensive glazing on the courtyard façade.

This cost-effective extension actually changes the complexion of the school: the original building now looks like the extension and the new addition like the main building. Combined with its elegant urban solution, this work proves the value of understatement.

Unfortunately, the architect was not able to do the same with the almost unnoticed and seldom-mentioned sports hall, located deep in the southwest corner of the courtyard. A very rational floor plan enables the building to function extremely well, but it lacks the flair of the ellipse. Instead, it sits as a large, squat box, penetrating deep into the courtyard and interrupting the free flow of space.

Stefan Scholz (BJSS) 1990

Kreuzberg to Neukölln

Stefan Scholz (BJSS) 1990

There may be many sports halls in Berlin that are superior to this one, but there is nothing to match the simple beauty of the ellipse of the school extension.

ADDRESS Parchimer Allee 125, Berlin-Neukölln [T–4]
CLIENT Bezirksamt Neukölln
STRUCTURAL ENGINEER Professor R L'Allemand and P Ludwig
COST DM 12 million
SIZE 14,744 cubic metres gross
U-BAHN Parchimer Allee
BUS 174
ACCESS open

Stefan Scholz (BJSS) 1990

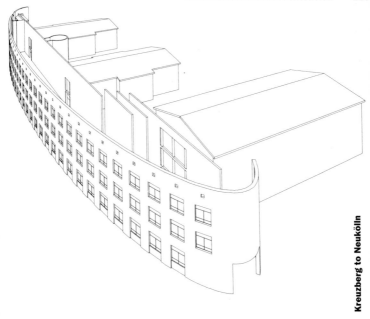

Stefan Scholz (BJSS) 1990

KITA, Buckower Damm

A grey-painted, concrete wall next to an auto-repair shop is all one can see from the busy street. The school itself is located deep inside the block where building land is cheap, with a narrow access as the only connnection with the outside world.

The architects have used the wall to connect the street with the school, incorporating a series of features and elements, such as pergolas and storage areas, along the way. Thus, this path becomes an integral part of the usable play area for the children as well.

The main building is a three-storey, brick-clad structure, with a glass and steel enclosed lift attached externally.

The interior is organised programatically with the service areas located to the east and the main classrooms to the west. The entire building is shoe-horned on to the site with little space in or around it. If one squeezes between the fence, trees and the building, a filigree steel and glass west façade can be seen. The image is striking, enhanced by the perspective. However, it is here that the building fails, for inadequate protection from the sun has led to bitter complaints among the members of staff about having to work and teach in a 'sauna'.

If and when adequate sun screens are provided, this building would become one of the most successful KITAS of recent years.

ADDRESS Buckower Damm 192, Berlin-Neukölln [T–3]
CLIENT Land Berlin
SIZE 1490 square metres
COST DM 6 million
U-BAHN Johannistaler Chaussee
BUS 144
ACCESS school hours

Kreuzberg to Neukölln

Büro Müller-Guilford 1992

Büro Müller-Guilford 1992

Primary school, Neuhofer Straße

Approached from the street, the dynamic form of the tower belies the true scale of this project.

The classrooms are arranged around a series of courtyards that bring natural light and ventilation deep inside the block and double up as an outdoor recreation and teaching space, depending upon the weather. The classrooms are hidden behind a series of brick arches as well as the rear wall of the covered bicycle stand area to protect them from the noise of the adjacent sports field. To the west, partially sunken into the earth, is the block containing the sports hall and its associated facilities. Windows to the south, west and east enable this space to enjoy good natural lighting, considering its depth below ground level.

The whole building is executed in a cavity-wall construction using a sand-coloured brick which gives the school a comfortable feeling, neither too heavy nor too massive.

The eye, however, is guided to the triangular tower of glass and render, and it is here where the problems of detailing are to be seen. Set apart from the ground floor by stilts and from the vertical circulation tower by 'bridges', this independent element is under constant repair due to the cracking render, and it is additionally reported that the roof continues to leak. Whether the fault of the designers or the builders, these problems serve as a warning to young architects.

ADDRESS Neuhofer Straße 41, Berlin-Neukölln [x–2]
CLIENT Bezirksamt Neukölln
COST DM 30 million (including exterior sports fields)
U-BAHN Rudow
BUS 271
ACCESS school hours

Brandt + Böttcher 1993

Brandt + Böttcher 1993

KITA, Groß-Ziethener-Chaussee

Three metal-clad triangular roof elements catch the eye as one nears the building. The rest of the children's day-care centre remains partially hidden by trees, fencing and playground equipment, making it difficult to obtain an overall view. Once this frustration is overcome, it is possible to discover a dense yet spacious composition.

The room programme is divided between a long narrow block which is intersected by three squares, each with attached quarter circles. These quarter circles contain rooms for the various children's groups, with each square serving as a multipurpose room for that area. The earth is modulated to allow light into the basement that contains the kitchen, dining, and sanitary facilities.

Built near to where the Wall once stood, this nursery school serves the myriad recently completed small-scale housing projects that have sprung up along the former death strip. Many are of considerable interest, including the white semi-detached villas located next door.

ADDRESS Groß-Ziethener-Chaussee 144, Berlin-Neukölln [v–1]
CLIENT Bezirksamt Neukölln
SIZE 2234 square metres
U-BAHN Rudow
BUS 271
ACCESS open 6.00–16.00

Deubzer König Architekten

Deubzer König Architekten

The Wall

BEWAG headquarters

This building complex for Berlin's electricity company is located directly adjacent to the former no-man's land, which has itself been turned into a park along the canal's edge.

Since reunification, the Schlesische Straße has become one of the main East–West links. Combined with the nearby s-Bahn station in the East and the U-Bahn station in the West, these offices literally pull together workers from both parts of the city.

The office programme is arranged in a series of blocks, interconnected by bridge elements. The blocks are grouped around a central entrance courtyard, and the wings project into the green space, creating pleasant views and thus avoiding the creation of a new wall along the water's edge.

The colour and quality of the brickwork is exquisite, as is the detailing.

The maturity of the trees allows the buildings to sit comfortably in the landscape without being in any way overpowering. Of note is the nearby surviving watch tower, formerly occupied by East German border guards. This structure has been converted into a mini-museum and is an integral element of the park.

ADDRESS Puschkinallee 52, Berlin-Treptow [U–8]
CLIENT Grundwertfond Schlesischer Busch, GbR
SIZE 46,000 square metres net
S-BAHN Schlesisches Tor
U-BAHN Treptower Park
BUS 166, 167, 265
ACCESS limited

The Wall

Liepe + Steigelmann 1995

Liepe + Steigelmann 1995

Oberbaumbrücke

Like Tower Bridge in London, Oberbaumbrücke symbolised the eastern entrance to the historical core of Berlin. Built in 1896, this neo-gothic brick structure originally accommodated not only normal street traffic, but also the new overground railway line via an arcade, an elegant asymmetrical solution for a then modern transport system. During the last days of the Second World War the central bay was blown up, and much of the bridge reduced to rubble. During the 1950s a provisional steel structure spanned the gap. With the building of the Wall, a checkpoint for West Berliners only was located on the bridge; occasionally a lone elderly pedestrian could be seen crossing among the ruins.

In 1992, the bridge started to be disassembled brick by brick down to the level of the main arches. Divers searched the river bed for fragments that could be reintegrated into the bridge or could serve as a model for some of the 460 different types of specially made brick forms.

A new reinforced-concrete bed was poured, which not only supports the increased weight of modern vehicles but also distributes the forces of the overhead railway. The arcade contains within the brickwork new steel beams and columns.

A new steel arch designed by Santiago Calatrava replaces the 1950s central bay. This modern intervention into the decorative brickwork is restrained yet elegant, a beautiful, subtle example of modern engineering enhancing a historical structure.

ADDRESS Oberbaumbrücke, Berlin-Friedrichshain [T–9]
S-BAHN Warschauer Straße
U-BAHN Schlesiches Tor, Warschauer Straße
BUS 147
ACCESS open

The Wall

Santiago Calatrava 1996

Santiago Calatrava 1996

The Wall

East Side Gallery

Created by numerous artists shortly after the collapse of the Communist regime, this section of the old 'inner wall' has now been listed as a historical landmark – a victory for art.

On its western side, the Berlin Wall was used as an outdoor art gallery for political and social criticism. Some of the murals were moving and penetrating; others, including a panel listing the names of Liverpool Football Club's squad, were quite humorous.

This section of the Wall was always painted white; no social criticism was allowed on its eastern face. Today, it is a wonderful open-air gallery attracting visitors from around the world. The famous 'Bruderkuss' of Honecker and Brezhnev is a must see.

However, time has already taken its toll; the paintings are deteriorating and the debate on whether to restore them or not is still on.

In the rapidly changing circumstances of Berlin, it is here that one can gain a feeling of what was in the air during the momentous weeks following 9 November 1989.

ADDRESS Mühlenstraße, Berlin-Friedrichshain [T-9]
BUILDER Erich Honecker
SIZE approximately 200 metres long
S-BAHN Warschauer Straße, Berlin Hauptbahnhof
U-BAHN Warschauer Straße
BUS 140, 142, 340
ACCESS open

The Wall

Various artists 1990

Various artists 1990

Offices at Hauptbahnhof

The pattern of locating large office complexes next to railway stations is continued here (see page 134). This complex is slightly different, however, due to the fact that the station is not located near the city centre but on its periphery. In addition, the immediate vicinity has none of the amenities usually associated with a high concentration of commuters, such as shops, cafés and bars. This unusual location is the site for the Berlin headquarters of one of Germany's largest banks.

The building itself takes up the entire block and incorporates an old school which has been remodelled into a much-needed hotel. A shopping passage has also been integrated into the block, providing the necessities. A rotunda topped by a glazed roof acts as the main entrance to the headquarters, thus creating an element representative of the bank's image and importance.

The entire structure is brick clad, with well-proportioned glazing elements piercing the wall. Though the complex as a whole has an overbearing appearance, it is the best bit of architecture in the area.

The surrounding district is now undergoing a regeneration with new shops and eating establishments springing up in the railway arches and in nearby old buildings. The platz in front of the headquarters and the existing department store is also scheduled for a facelift.

A catalyst for the area, this building is a bold stroke taken by a normally conservative organisation.

ADDRESS Koppenstraße, Langestraße, Berlin-Friedrichshain [T–10]
CLIENT Dresdner Bank
S-BAHN Hauptbahnhof
BUS 140, 142, 340
ACCESS open

The Wall

Fischer und Fischer 1996

The Wall

Fischer und Fischer 1996

DAZ

Hidden behind a second-hand car lot and difficult to find, the remains of a large warehouse complex have been converted into the Deutsches Architekten Zentrum (German Architecture Centre). On the lower floors are located exhibition space, conference rooms and a restaurant. Above are small offices and studios for architects and artists. In addition, various important architectural associations, such as the BDA (Society of German Architects), the BDI (Society of Interior Designers) and the BDL (Society of Landscape Architects), have chosen to locate their Berlin headquarters here, which has in turn had a synergetic effect on the architectural scene in the city.

The architect has successfully integrated old and new. Where possible, details have been restored or reinstated. A new plane of glass and steel closes the wound caused by the earlier demolition of part of the building. Inserted into this glass plane at ground level is the prefabricated, concrete cube that is the entrance.

The whole is carefully and confidently executed. DAZ is a perfect example of what can be achieved when young talent is given a chance.

ADDRESS Köpenicker Straße 48–49, Berlin-Kreuzberg [s–9]
S-BAHN Hauptbahnhof
BUS 140, 147
ACCESS open

The Wall

Claus Anderhalten 1995

The Wall

Claus Anderhalten 1995

Luisenstädtisher canal and garden

In 1852 a canal connecting the River Spree and the Landwehr Canal was opened. The canal and the block structure of the area were conceived by Peter-Joseph Lenée who regarded the canal as a stimulus to development and a part of a green belt. But it was too small, and there was usually more raw sewage floating about than water. In 1926 the canal was filled in and Erwin Barth designed a series of gardens to replace the water. Various landscapes were created which doubled as playgrounds for the by-then densely populated area. The gardens remained lower than the streets on either side, creating a strong linear axis and identity.

After 1945 a lot of rubble was unthinkingly dumped into the 'ditch' and covered over. Only fragments of the park remained. The building of the Wall in 1961 cut this park in half with the West partially restoring it and the East using it as a ready-made death strip.

Today, excavations have revealed a tremendous amount of the original substance and it is planned to restore, where possible, the 1926 conditions. Where only bits remain, they will be integrated into new pieces of landscape design. St Michael's church will regain its place as the element which turns the axis through the soon-to-be-restored reflecting pool.

A major meeting point for the formerly divided communities will thus be regained where only a few years ago no-one dared to go.

ADDRESS Wassertorplatz, Oranienplatz, H Heine Platz, Schillingbrücke, Berlin-Kreuzberg, Berlin-Mitte [s–9]
CLIENT Senatsverwaltung für Stadtentwiklung und Umweltschutz
S-BAHN Jannowitzbrücke, Berlin Hauptbahnhof
U-BAHN Moritzplatz, Kottbusser Tor
BUS 140, 147
ACCESS open

The Wall

Horst Schumacher 1995

TRIAS

One of the most photogenic projects of recent years, this is a welcome relief from the excesses of critical reconstruction.

The Holzmarktstraße is a major artery full of heavy and noisy traffic leading into the city centre. Sandwiched in between the street and the overground railway arches, the site has few connections with the area around it.

The architects made the conscious decision to make the most of this leftover site by erecting an object – one that in itself makes the site valuable and desirable – rather than trying to repair or mend the surrounding area.

The result is a six-storey block along the street, in scale with the buildings nearby. The stroke of genius was the carving up of the bulk of the office accommodation into three curving towers, each containing 13 storeys. This allows all the offices to have spectacular views of the river and thus to all command premium rents.

The green-tinted glazing, along with the curving form, softens the scale of these otherwise conventionally built towers, endowing them with an unusual elegance, especially when viewed at an angle from across the river.

ADDRESS Holzmarktstraße 15–18, Berlin-Mitte [S–10]
CLIENT DG Anlage GmbH
SIZE 25,000 square metres
S-BAHN Janowitzbrücke
BUS 240
ACCESS open

The Wall

Berginger + Wawrick 1996

The Wall

Berginger + Wawrick 1996

Jannowitz Centre

For many years not only the Wall divided Berlin, but the river as well. Thus, even on the West Berlin side, the Spree had become a little used transport link, of no consequence and no value. Coupled with the general decline of inner-city harbours through deindustrialisation and DDR misindustrialisation, the river edge was neglected and fell into disrepair. It was only with reunification that the possibilities for future developments along the Spree began to be realised.

The Jannowitz Centre, located directly at the corner of a bridge which relinks East and West Berlin, is a dense development of office and commercial space. The design is a series of rectangular blocks running parallel to the river. A glass structure placed at the perpendicular creates a series of atriums between the individual blocks. The atriums add a transparence and lightness to the complex and allow the passerby a view into its internal organisation and life.

Surprisingly, in spite of the area's dense, dirty, and extremely loud setting, the Federal Ministry of the Environment has chosen to locate its new offices here, continuing the recent trend, in this era of budgetary restraints, for the government to favour rental accommodation above purpose-built structures.

ADDRESS Brückenstraße, Berlin-Mitte [s–10]
CLIENT Holzmann Bauprojekt AG Berlin
SIZE 30,000 square metres
S-BAHN Jannowitzbrücke
BUS 240
ACCESS limited

The Wall

Hentrich-Petschnigg + Partner 1997

The Wall

Hentrich-Petschnigg + Partner 1997

Federal Printing Works

This block was heavily damaged during the war. Afterwards the construction of the Wall prevented the corner from being redeveloped, the Wall's edge being in fact that of the pavement, making vehicle access impossible. With the removal of the Wall, access to the adjacent streets was restored, placing the building in a prime location.

The block's edges and traditional eaves heights have been reinstated but, unlike elsewhere, the architecture has not been constrained by the dictates of critical reconstruction. Instead, it is vibrant, even exhilarating. A variety of architectural expression is brought to the development, for here, unusually, there are several investors at work.

The first project by BHHS and Partner is the extension of the Federal Printing Works along the Kommandantenstraße. The building programme is clearly defined: the office track is placed along the street front, with storage areas running parallel behind. The storage facility is constructed so as to integrate the three-point, steel-arch structural system that spans the production hall, allowing a column-free floor area of over 2300 square metres. Located deeper in the block are additional building volumes which house special functions including studios for engravers and graphic designers.

The second project, which was designed by Krug & Partner, is the Berlin headquarters of the Society for Auto Mechanics. The façade is dominated by a wall of sound-insulating glass hung a metre in front of the office accommodation. The set-back roof storey accommodates three apartments, and a bistro and shop are located on the ground floor, reflecting Berlin's traditional programmatic mixture.

A third project, produced by Rupert Ahlborn und Partner, is for a new office building and the renovation and restoration of its neighbour in the Lindenstraße. Also of note is the conversion of Lindenstraße 40–41 by

BHHS und Partner

BHHS und Partner

Marion Drews into a youth centre. The inner courtyard with its modernist bridge linking the two wings is worth a look. It is best seen when walking through and under.

Taken as a whole, the block is successful at a city-planning level as well as architecturally. It shows that modern architecture can still respond to the challenge of contributing to the urban environment.

ADDRESS Kommandantenstraße/Lindenstraße, Berlin-Kreuzberg [R–9]
ASSOCIATED ARCHITECTS Rupert Alhborn und Partner (BEK headquarters); Marion Drews (youth centre); Krug & Partner (Society for Auto Mechanics)
U-BAHN Spittelmarkt
BUS 129, 141
ACCESS limited

The Wall

BHHS und Partner

BHHS und Partner

Mosse-Zentrum

Very few knew that this masterpiece still existed. Located next to the Wall in the East, the area was seldom visited by either Westerners or Easterners. Damaged in the war and later stripped of its ornament, it was hardly recognisable. However, as part of a new publishing centre, Erich Mendelsohn's famous conversion has now been restored.

In 1921, Mendelsohn was asked to add storeys to the publishing house's headquarters. He not only provided the extra space, but also extended the addition down to the ground at the corner, thus giving the building an entirely new character – modern, sleek and powerful. Unfortunately, much of this original building was lost. War damage and subsequent socialist planning also removed the surrounding context and therefore much of the project's original power. To complete the block, a huge new addition has been added. Although it respects the traditional 22-metre eaves line, it otherwise makes no attempt at historicisation; it is clean and modern, well-proportioned with well-executed detailing.

These two projects are additional steps in the re-establishment of this area as Berlin's publishing centre.

ADDRESS Schützenstraße 15–17, Berlin-Mitte [Q–9]
CLIENT Druckhaus Berlin Mitte GmbH
ORIGINAL ARCHITECT Erich Mendelsohn
COST DM 370 million
SIZE 60,000 square metres
U-BAHN Kochstraße
BUS 129, 142, 147
ACCESS open

The Wall

Bernd Kemper (restoration) and Fissler-Ernst (new offices)

Bernd Kemper (restoration) and Fissler-Ernst (new offices)

Schützenquartier

This particular block had been extensively damaged – first by bombing raids, then by house-to-house street fighting, and finally by the building of the Wall – so much so that only one building in the Schützenstraße has survived to this day.

In his planning of this area, Rossi's approach has been very different to that applied to other nearby office and commercial projects. He has proposed the reinstatement of the old plots, including the small courtyards within the block's interior. No gimmicky atriums or shopping passages are used, instead the successful urban tradition of Berlin will be restored.

The breakdown of the block into small individual plots will also allow each building's façade to be handled separately, ensuring variety. Again, this is a refreshing departure from other recent developments where a single massive office building dominates the entire block.

Unfortunately, the current designs show an overpreponderance of colour, which could turn the composition into a circus if care and restraint are not exercised. Otherwise, for the way in which it sets out to repair Berlin's urban fabric, this project has the potential to be one of the more successful developments.

ADDRESS Schützenstraße, Markgrafenstraße, Zimmerstraße, Charlottenstraße, Berlin-Mitte [Q–9]
CLIENT Dr Peter and Isolde Kottmair GbR
ASSOCIATED ARCHITECTS Götz Bellmann and Walter Böhm; Luca Meda
U-BAHN Stadtmitte
BUS 129
ACCESS under construction

The Wall

Aldo Rossi

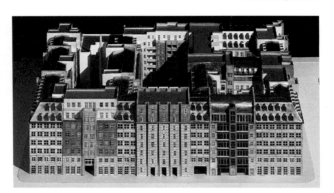

The Wall

Aldo Rossi

Offices, Charlottenstraße

Unnoticed in the hullabaloo surrounding the planned developments at Checkpoint Charlie and in the Friedrichstraße, this building does more to repair the historical structure of this area than any of them.

Situated directly in the former death strip of the Berlin Wall, these offices re-establish the corner and street lines of the ravaged block. The building's massing is broken down by treating it as if it were in fact three separate buildings: a cube with a square roof tower emphasising the corner, and two side buildings with receding barrel-vaulted roofs.

Shops at street level will help to bring life back to this devastated area. Provision for parking has been made through the construction of a fully automatic underground car park with special lifts for the vehicles.

Similar small-scale interventions or repairs of this type – rather than the mega projects which are planned to surround it – would make Berlin a much more dynamic and exciting city.

ADDRESS Charlottenstraße 80, Berlin-Mitte [Q–9]
CLIENT H + W Vermögens und Verwaltung GbR
STRUCTURAL ENGINEER Krüger und Partner
COST DM 25 million
SIZE 5400 square metres of lettable space
U-BAHN Kochstraße
BUS 129, 142, 147
ACCESS open

The Wall

Arno Bonanni and Klaus Lattermann 1994

The Wall

Arno Bonanni and Klaus Lattermann 1994

Office building, Zimmerstraße

The Zimmerstraße itself used to be located entirely within the death strip. The buildings to the north belonged to East Berlin, those to the south to West Berlin. However, due to war damage, not a single structure along the south street edge was left standing.

Instead of trying to recreate a series of smaller buildings with the proportions of a traditional street-frontage, the architect has proposed a bold but simple solution. A long, seven-storey building, marked at each end by a ship-shape tower, attaches itself to the remaining original structures, thus completing the block.

Clear and rational, this façade makes no historical references. It appears to be a modern building in the truest sense.

The success of this building is due to the way in which it repairs the urban fabric in a simple, straightforward manner – proof that rational modern architecture can peacefully coexist with the city-planning goals of critical reconstruction. Why then does this not apply to Pariser Platz (see page 190)?

ADDRESS Zimmerstraße, Berlin-Kreuzberg [Q–9]
U-BAHN Kochstraße
BUS 129
ACCESS open

The Wall

Professor Josef P Kleihues 1995

The Wall

Professor Josef P Kleihues 1995

House at Checkpoint Charlie

It is only fitting that the Office for Metropolitan Architecture was commissioned to design this building at such a unique and challenging site. OMA expounds a powerful philosophy. It believes that through the collision of the forces that are active in an urban situation, new architectural solutions and forms can be generated that go exponentially beyond the brief, adding new elements and dynamism to city life.

Their response here was an immediate rejection of any reference to the adjoining buildings and existing street lines. Instead, the building is set back from the street and its height is determined by its own needs and functions.

In the original built version, the ground level was designed as the new American checkpoint. A yellow control box cantilevered out over the pavement, marking the entrance for motor vehicles. Once inside, the drivers, their cargo and papers were to be processed and thrust out again between a nautilus and boomerang curve. Above the checkpoint, two stacks of two-level terraced housing were provided. The roof of the rear of the checkpoint acted as their private gardens. Above that, accessed by a screened exterior, conventional flats were located. The roof level contains a series of penthouses while the roof itself cantilevers out and over the façade, making its announcement to those arriving from East Berlin.

Both the site and the programme are dense. The building combined a unique ground-floor usage with the attempt to make housing attractive, not through softness or green space, but through its very hardness and unique juxtaposition.

Sadly for this building, the Wall came down before the Americans could move in. Since then, a series of boring shop fronts have been inserted at ground level; these project out and re-establish the old street edge.

The Wall

Office for Metropolitan Architecture 1989

Office for Metropolitan Architecture 1989

This is still a powerful building, hard and imposing. It is a building conceived for a divided city and for this unique site. With the bizarreness of the situation gone, it has lost its magic. This is the only instance I know of where the Berlin Wall is sorely missed.

ADDRESS Friedrichstraße 207–208, Berlin-Kreuzberg [Q–9]
CLIENT Berlin Eigenheimbau GmbH
COST DM 7.5 million
U-BAHN Kochstraße
BUS 129
ACCESS open

The Wall

Office for Metropolitan Architecture 1989

Office for Metropolitan Architecture 1989

Checkpoint Charlie – the Business Centre and Triangle

Probably most famous for being the site where Soviet and American tanks faced off each other in August 1961, Checkpoint Charlie has achieved legendary status.

In reality, Checkpoint Charlie was nothing more than a Portakabin housing a few US marines in the middle of a narrow street.

'Checkpoint Charlie – the Business Centre' is actually planned on land that was entirely on the East Berlin side of the Wall. The eastern side had been devastated not only by the war, but by the razing of buildings to provide better sightlines to prevent escapes. A large area had been covered with a sheet-metal roof, under which were various buildings for East German borderguards, police and customs officials who would inspect vehicles, their occupants' papers as well as cargo, human or otherwise. To the east edge of the compound, a series of interconnected barracks was set up to handle the pedestrian traffic.

Shortly before the Americans were to move into their just-completed installation within the OMA Checkpoint Charlie building, the Berlin Wall came down. Within 11 months, reunification had taken place and amid great ceremony the Portakabin that had served as the Allied checkpoint was closed and carted away to a museum on the other side of town. The East German installation was also then disassembled, except for a guard tower which today remains a point of contention between the developer and the local museum.

The brainchild of a former US diplomat and banker, the Business Centre in its planning re-establishes the historic street pattern of prewar Berlin. The site was divided into blocks and several leading German and American architectural firms were selected through an invited competition.

The selected firms included Philip Johnson Architects (Quartier 106),

Various architects

The Wall

Various architects

Jürgen Engel (Quartier 200), Lauber und Wöhr (Quartier 201A), and Glass und Bender (Quartier 201B). The most interesting of the proposals came from David Childs of Skidmore Owings & Merrill (Quartier 105).

Set on a tiny piece of land that does not belong to the Checkpoint Charlie development, an office building by Josef P Kleihues (named the 'Triangle') is nearing completion. The triangular site dictates the floor plan and stairs and WCs are all located in the very centre, allowing the office space to run uninterrupted around the edges of the building. Although granite cladding is used, the architecture is rational and modern.

The entire complex, lost in the intense publicity surrounding Potsdamer Platz, will actually do more to tie together seamlessly East and West than its competitor.

ADDRESS Friedrichstraße between Leipziger Platz and Kochstraße, Berlin-Mitte [Q–9]
CLIENT American Business Centre GmbH + Co, Checkpoint KG (Business Centre); TCHA Grundstücke Berlin GbR (Triangle)
COST DM 1.1 thousand million (Business Centre)
SIZE 115,000 square metres (Business Centre)
U-BAHN Kochstraße, Stadtmitte
BUS 129, 147

The Wall

Various architects

Quartier 106
Philip-Johnson-Haus

Various architects

Copper strip

The Wall couldn't be torn down quickly enough: now everyone is trying to put it up again. West Berliners have a love-hate relationship with it; almost all discussions concerning the erection of memorials and historical markers are dominated by the *Wessis* (West Germans). The wall to the Easterners was a forbidden zone, out of sight; it was therefore pushed back into the subconscious. There was neither a need nor a desire to document it.

Amid the various monumental, fanciful, and just plain idiotic concepts bantered about is one that is so simple and elegant that one is amazed that it has actually been built.

A 7-centimetre-wide copper strip with the inscription 'Berlin Wall 1961–1989' has been laid along a stretch of where the Wall used to run. The material itself differentiates it from all other street markings, and the fact that it is level with the ground avoids any debates about three-dimensional interventions into the space around it.

The design marks the position of the Wall, but it is politically neutral. What one derives out of it is based upon one's relationship to the Wall.

To date, only a small portion has been installed. The debate over its cost and extension (documenting the entire length of the Wall) is ongoing.

The Wall

ADDRESS Niederkirchner Straße between Martin-Gropius-Bau and Abgeordnetenhaus, Berlin-Kreuzberg [P–9]
U-BAHN Kochstraße, Potsdamer Platz
BUS 129
ACCESS open

Potsdamer Platz

The 1920s were the golden age of Potsdamer Platz. With the nearby Potsdamer and Anhalter train stations, it was the pulsating heart of Berlin. Devastated by war, insurrection and the building of the Wall, Berlin's heart ceased to beat.

Berlin became a New York without Times Square, a London without Trafalgar Square. The divided sectors looked inwards for their own individual centres. The East to Alexanderplatz, the West to the Ku'damm. Potsdamer Platz, where East and West met, was left to rot; its only inhabitants were wild rabbits and borderguards.

After the fall of the Berlin Wall, all eyes turned again to Potsdamer Platz. An international city-planning ideas competition was held in 1991, with the German practice of Hilmer und Sattler winning first prize. Their proposal envisaged restoring the historic street plan as much as possible in the area. In order to maintain a sense of scale, the buildings were broken into a series of small independent cubes to allow flexibility in ownership and rentability.

The Berlin government, however, sold the land not to several small developers, but to just three very large concerns (Sony, A+T and Daimler-Benz) at dumping prices. Each company organised their own invited competition, with the following results – Daimler-Benz: Renzo Piano; Sony: Helmut Jahn; A+T: Giorgio Grassi. Each of these winners modified the Hilmer and Sattler plan to a certain extent, and appointed other individual architects to design many of the buildings.

The problems of infrastructure and traffic management have had to be co-ordinated among all involved in and around Potsdamer Platz, as well as with the federal and city governments. A new main train station for all of Berlin is planned for Lehrter Bahnhof, to the north across the river. A new rail tunnel for local trains will connect this station with Pots-

The Wall

Hilmer und Sattler (plan) 1991

The Wall

Hilmer und Sattler (plan) 1991

damer Platz. At the moment, one underground and one s-Bahn line already serve Potsdamer Platz, with a third being planned.

A road tunnel is also under construction, linking the area north of the Spree with a main East–West artery along the canal in the south.

Although costing only a tenth as much per kilometre to build and maintain as the u-Bahn, only one tram line is currently planned to serve the Potsdamer Platz development.

The logistics of the building site are themselves interesting. South of the canal, a large compound has been set up, railway tracks laid, a loading and unloading terminal – capable of handling the immense volume of earth that needs to be excavated as well as the building material needed to erect the structures – has been built, and a factory producing concrete just for this site is in place. A new service road and bridge have been built to link the compound with the site in order to avoid the construction vehicles getting tied up in traffic.

A gigantic publicity campaign has been launched, keeping the press and public fully informed about each new event happening on site. Guided tours of the site played a major part in Berlin's summer 1996 festival. The erection of the Info Box (see page 176) was a stroke of genius; everyone is waiting with anticipation for the completion of the project. However, when one carefully studies the glossy brochures, one realises that although many of the buildings will be architectural masterpieces, the scale and density will be extremely overpowering.

ADDRESS Potsdamer Platz, Berlin-Tiergarten [P–9]
U-BAHN Potsdamer Platz
S-BAHN Potsdamer Platz
BUS 142, 348

The Wall

Hilmer und Sattler (plan) 1991

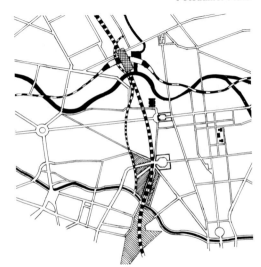

s-Bahn
Tunnels
River/canal
Major streets

Potsdamer Platz
Logistics centre
New train station

Hilmer und Sattler (plan) 1991

Info Box

Probably Berlin's best-known new building, the Info Box is the first completed structure of the Potsdamer Platz development. Designed to stand out among the chaos of building cranes and concrete, this signal-red container acts as a magnet for tourists visiting the site.

Actually located on Leipziger Platz, the Info Box contains over 1000 square metres of exhibition space.

Sony, A+T and Daimler-Benz, as well as all others involved with Potsdamer Platz, are represented. A restaurant and souvenir shop are also located within the Box's steel-panelled walls, with major functions, including private parties, catered for in a special events space.

The whole building has been designed to be easily dismantled and erected elsewhere. As the subject of several architectural and industry-related awards, however, many feel it should remain as part of the rebuilt Leipziger Platz, serving as a multipurpose building – or even as a piece of art.

Detailed information about the Potsdamer Platz development and this structure can best be obtained from the bookstore on the first floor.

ADDRESS Leipziger Platz 21, Berlin-Mitte [P–9]
COST DM 10 million
SIZE 2,200 square metres gross
U-BAHN Potsdamer Platz
S-BAHN Potsdamer Platz
BUS 142, 348
ACCESS daily 9.00–19.00, Thursday 9.00–21.00

The Wall

Schneider und Schumacher

The Wall

Schneider und Schumacher

Daimler-Benz

With 19 planned buildings, this is the largest of the three projects in the Potsdamer Platz development. Though half of the space is allocated to offices, a fifth is housing and the rest is given over to shops, restaurants, a hotel, a musical-variety theatre and a Cinemax centre. The Renzo Piano Building Workshop, together with Christoph Kohlbecker, are responsible for the overall co-ordination of the scheme. As well as producing their own designs, they have invited several well-known architects to participate in the project. The most outstanding proposals are Richard Rogers' office blocks (pictured below) and Renzo Piano's 3-D cinema. The first structures scheduled for completion are the two office buildings by Arata Isozaki and Renzo Piano. Projected finish date is 1998.

It remains to be seen if this project will be successful at the urban level; many believe that the streets will be dead after 18.00 The inclusion of entertainment facilities and housing is intended to mitigate this fear.

ADDRESS Potsdamer Straße, Kemperplatz, Berlin-Tiergarten [P–9]
CLIENT Daimler-Benz, Interservices (debis)
ASSOCIATED ARCHITECT Christoph Kohlbecker
SIZE 34,000 square metres above ground level
U-BAHN Potsdamer Platz
S-BAHN Potsdamer Platz
BUS 142, 348

The Wall

Renzo Piano Building Workshop et al 1996–98

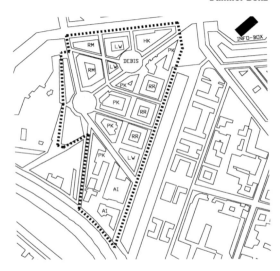

AI Arata Isozaki
HK Hans Kollhoff
L+W Lauber + Wöhr

P+K Piano + Kohlbecker
RM Rafael Moneo
RR Richard Rogers

The Wall

Renzo Piano Building Workshop et al 1996–98

Sony

Helmut Jahn chose to break with Hilmer and Sattler's masterplan by making the site into one giant block, with no streets running across or through it. Instead, he has planned a raised plinth over most of the site, with separate buildings above and below it.

The financial backbone of the project is of course office space, located in the various buildings along the former Entlastungsstraße, including Sony's own European headquarters. A 26-storey office tower directly on Potsdamer Platz helps build the gateway between East and West.

Apartments, a fifth of the development, are located in two blocks, one ringing the main elliptical space, the other along the Bellevue Straße. This building is of particular note since it incorporates parts of the historical Esplanade Hotel that survived the war, including the famous so-called Kaisersaal and breakfast rooms. In a very complicated and highly publicised event, these rooms (weighing 1300 tonnes) were moved 75 metres over a new concrete bed using compressed air.

The heart of the project is the 'Forum', a 4000-square-metre elliptical arena covered by a fibreglass membrane. Shops and restaurants are located at the edges, with an IMAX 3-D cinema, a German Mediathek, a Filmhouse and a multiplex movie centre, the latter being located under the Forum itself.

Unlike the other projects, Sony is a self-contained world, combining work, home and entertainment under one roof.

ADDRESS Potsdamer Straße, Bellevue Straße, Kemperplatz, Berlin-Tiergarten [P–9]
U-BAHN Potsdamer Platz
S-BAHN Potsdamer Platz
BUS 142, 348

Helmut Jahn 1996–99

The Wall

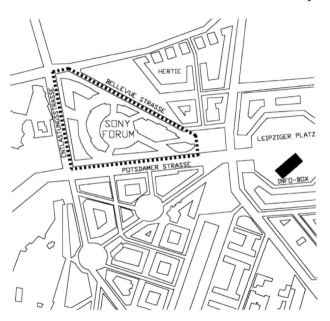

Helmut Jahn 1996–99

This development is completely different from the other two Potsdamer Platz projects in its approach to architecture. Produced under the direction of Giorgio Grassi, it reminds one immediately of the paintings of the Italian surrealist Giorgio de Chirico.

All five buildings are clad in red brickwork, with holes punched in for windows in a vertical format in a monotonous grid. Except for the loggias of the L-shaped housing blocks to the south, there is no real differentiation in the façades of the buildings.

The rounded 12-storey building towards Potsdamer Platz is intended to evoke the famous Haus Vaterland building that once stood on this site, but fails miserably.

Even the glossy promotional brochures depict melancholy structures amid blue skies and green trees. One hates to think how this development will look on a typical November day.

The Wall

ADDRESS Köthener Straße, Berlin-Tiergarten [P–9]
CLIENT ABB + Terrano
S-BAHN Potsdamer Platz, Anhalter Bahnhof
BUS 341

Giorgio Grassi et al 1996–99

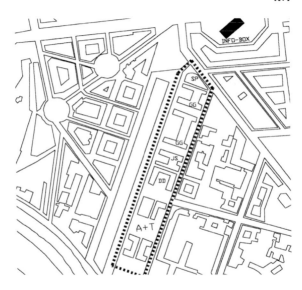

SP Schweger + Partner
GG Giorgio Grassi

JS Jürgen Sawade
DD Diener + Diener

Giorgio Grassi et al 1996–99

The Wall

Potsdamer Straße 1

Not to be found at the Info Box is information concerning the development of the north edge of Potsdamer Platz, the Hertie and Delbrück site.

Currently, a 23-storey glass and steel tower is planned at the corner, with a 10-storey-base building occupying the rest of the site. Little is known of its progress, but it raises an important point: how will the major projects work in an urban context if some sites (including Leipziger Platz) are developed later, or not at all?

ADDRESS Potsdamer Straße 1, Berlin-Tiergarten [P–10]
U-BAHN Potsdamer Platz
S-BAHN Potsdamer Platz
BUS 142, 348

The Wall

Sievers + Piatscheck + Partner

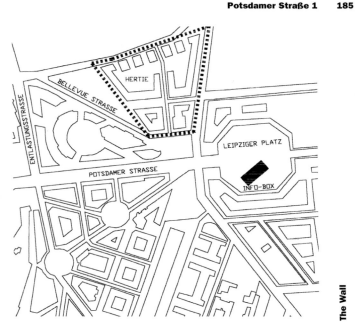

Sievers + Piatscheck + Partner

Leipziger Platz

The octagonal platz was once one of the most beautiful of all Berlin's public spaces. The development here will be of a totally different architectural nature from that of the high-profile Potsdamer and Pariser Platz. Aldo Rossi is responsible for the masterplan of the northwest corner, a site originally occupied by Alfred Messel's magnificent Wertheim department store. Rossi has rejected the temptation to recreate the past; instead, he has subdivided the block into small parcels which will be designed individually by various architects. The programme calls for a wide spectrum of usages: government offices, a hotel and, in the centre, a new theatre for the internationally renowned Cirque de Soleil. A large golden dome over the theatre will mark the complex, giving Berlin's skyline an exciting new element.

Next door at Leipziger Platz 15, a new office block – Mosse Palais, designed by HDS + Gallagher – is currently under construction. It is located on the site of a house of the same name which was torn down with the building of the Wall. For the time being, however, an official stop order has halted construction work as the building department and owners are unable to agree over the density ratio.

ADDRESS Leipziger Platz 12–13, 124–137, Berlin-Mitte [P–9]
CLIENTS Dr Peter and Isolde Kottmair (Leipziger Platz); DBM Holding (Mosse Palais)
SIZE 234,000 square metres (Leipziger Platz); 9000 square metres (Mosse Palais)
S-BAHN Potsdamer Platz
U-BAHN Potsdamer Platz
BUS 142, 348

The Wall

Aldo Rossi (masterplan)

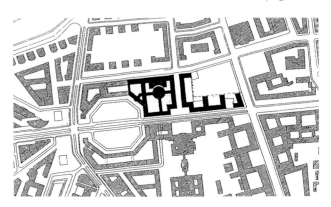

Aldo Rossi (masterplan)

Ministers' Garden

Two controversial projects are being planned on the site of the former Ministergarden: offices for representatives from each federal state government, and 'A Memorial to the Murdered Jews of Europe'. The area between Leipziger Platz and the Pariser Platz is to be divided into three blocks: the southernmost containing a series of villas housing the representatives will complete the block structure; the central block is to have villas only along the south edge, creating an unresolved no-man's land; and the northern block is reserved for the memorial.

However, several states are resisting the move from Bonn to Berlin. A further contention is the integration of the existing precast housing block.

The controversy around the memorial is more complex. Two first prizes were awarded. Simon Ungers proposed a large square enclosed by raised steel beams symbolising rails. Each rail would have the names of different concentration camps perforated in mirror-image, the names projected by sunlight on the square itself amid the black shadow cast by the rails. The other first prize, produced by a team of Berlin artists, envisaged a gigantic tilted square in which the individual names of the victims would be engraved. Chancellor Kohl intervened personally to stop the project, objecting to the sheer size and inadequacy of the designs. Both are huge in scale and totally inappropriate to the location.

The idea of holding a new competition is now being discussed.

ADDRESS No-man's land atop the Führerbunker between Leipziger Platz and Behrenstraße, Berlin-Mitte [P–9]
B-PLAN Dubach und Kohlbrenner
U-BAHN Potsdamer Platz
BUS 142, 348
ACCESS open

The Wall

Machleidt + Partner

A Ministers' Garden
B Memorial to the
  Murdered Jews of
  Europe
C Pariser Platz
D Leipziger Platz
E Tiergarten

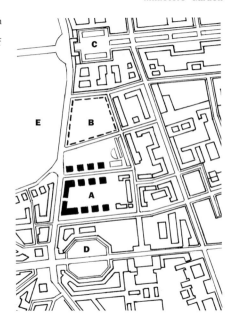

Machleidt + Partner

Pariser Platz

Originally, the Pariser Platz around the Brandenburg Gate was a proper square lined with prestigious buildings. Until recently, due to the war and the Wall, the Brandenburg Gate stood as an isolated monument, the best-known symbol of the cold war. After reunification, an intense debate raged as to how the platz should be treated: to rebuild true to the original, or to create a traffic circle around the gate like the Arc de Triomphe in Paris? In keeping with the worst of Berlin's traditions, it was decided to please no one by not offending anyone: a compromise was reached. The original building lines and the square were to be reinstated, with few exceptions. However, the façades of the buildings could be modern, although there were certain restrictions. Even more bizarre was the decision to reinstate the street but not to permit traffic.

Surprisingly, there are glimmers of hope. Several architects have chosen to bend or break the rules of critical reconstruction, notably Behnisch for the Academy of Art. Others – such as Gehry, Moore Ruble Yudell and von Gerkan, Marg und Partner – have focused on the creation of exciting interior spaces while respecting the stringent external restrictions.

Great buildings need a banal background in order to stand out. This has been adequately provided by the architects of the other buildings. Ranging from the bland to historical pastiche, they at least complete the platz by defining its edges and giving the whole a sense of place.

As elsewhere in Berlin, critical reconstruction will succeed in re-establishing Berlin's lost sense of urbanism, but any architectural success will be achieved only by those architects who reach beyond it.

ADDRESS Pariser Platz, Berlin-Mitte [P–10]
S-BAHN Unter den Linden
BUS 100, 147, 346

The Wall

Various architects 1997–2000

Various architects 1997–2000

HAUS SOMMER, PARISER PLATZ 1 (Professor Josef P Kleihues)
Originally this house and its twin to the north butted directly up against the Brandenburg Gate. Each comprising 11 bays and three storeys, the eaves lines of these buildings respected the cornices of their neighbours. Late classical ornamentation decorated the façades and formed an unobtrusive backdrop to the gate.

Kleihues has kept the eaves height, but now the buildings comprise four storeys and only ten bays, leaving a gap between themselves and the gate. The stone cladding is in keeping with the original but all ornamentation has been left out. Many argued that replicas of the originals should have been built; others championed a truly modern interpretation. What is being constructed is neither one nor the other. They are a bland backdrop to the gate, exactly what Haus Sommer and Liebermann were originally.

US EMBASSY, PARISER PLATZ 2 (Moore Ruble Yudell; completion 1999)
The Americans never had much luck with this site: the original privately used building burnt in 1930 and was reconstructed as the embassy, opening in 1939 just in time for the outbreak of the Second World War. Heavily damaged, it was ripped down during the 1950s. After the construction of the Wall the property became unavailable for use since it lay in the middle of no-man's land.

The architects, winners of an invited competition, proposed organising the massive building programme around a central courtyard. The entrance would be located not at the front but within the courtyard, with the façade towards the platz being broken in two, in a way that is unexpected and unforeseen by the zoning codes. The initial perspectives indicate a delicate and light handling of the stone-clad façades, which are broken down into base, middle and cornice/roof elements.

The Wall

Various architects 1997–2000

Professor Josef P Kleihues

DG BANK, PARISER PLATZ 3 (Frank O Gehry and Associates)
Frank Gehry's compliance with the zoning codes, which require a stone
façade with vertical holes punched in it for windows, was totally unexpected. Behind this screen, Gehry has proposed a rigid, almost symmet-
rical plan. He uses this rigidity to play off the free forms he has created
for various programmatic elements, including the conference rooms. The
atrium roof is also broken into a series of jagged forms, increasing in
height from the five storeys of banking accommodated towards the platz
to ten storeys of housing located along the Behrenstraße.

The design recognises the limitations imposed by outside forces, and
then rises above them.

AKADEMIE DER KUNSTE, PARISER PLATZ 4 (Günter Behnisch)
Only the rear portion of the Academy of Art survived the war and the
Wall. It is the last remaining original structure on Pariser Platz.

The debate surrounding this building does not involve Behnisch's
proposal to incorporate the old and the new: all recognise the quality of
his spatial arrangements and plans. The storm rages over his façade. The
zoning codes require windows to be in a vertical format and the façade
to be at least 50 per cent solid. The architect reinterpreted the old historical façade by abstracting its proportions through the use of glass and
steel. Although initially approved, permission has been revoked by the
new building senator. The Academy and Behnisch are continuing to fight
against this ruling, and the situation remains unresolved.

ADLON HOTEL, UNTER DEN LINDEN 75–77 (Patzschke, Klotz und Partner)
The original Adlon Hotel, built in 1907, was conceived as a rival to the
grand hotels of Europe. It was to be a place for the great, the rich and

Various architects 1997–2000

The Wall

Professor Josef P Kleihues

the famous. Leading artists, politicians, industrialists and members of royalty were all a part of the Adlon legend.

After the war, the remnants were pulled down as part of the 'improvements' carried out to no-man's land and the Wall. Although the DDR had worked up proposals to rebuild it, the site lay empty until now.

Seizing the opportunity created by reunification, an investor signed a deal with Berlin's leading hotel group to rebuild the Adlon. Unfortunately, it will not be a faithful reconstruction of the original building, but merely a pastiche based on a loose interpretation, an architectural rival, at best, to the DDR's monstrous Grand Hotel in the Friedrichstraße.

One advantage it does have over its rival is location. Marketing will determine its success.

DRESDNER BANK, PARISER PLATZ 5A–6 (von Gerkan, Marg und Partner)
Before the war two separate buildings occupied the site; one even survived into the early 1960s. However, due to the construction of the Wall, it was demolished and the site was left vacant until now.

The German architects von Gerkan, Marg und Partner won the invited competition for the construction of new premises for the Dresdner Bank. Because the site is bounded on three sides by neighbouring buildings, the architects proposed arranging most of the offices around a glazed atrium of 29 metres in diameter.

The façade complies with the zoning codes that require stone cladding with punched holes for windows in a vertical format. The only decoration *per se* is the set-back entrance with its rounded edges trimmed in bronze.

As with most other buildings on Pariser Platz, the main architectural feature of the bank will be the quality of its interior space.

The Wall

Various architects 1997–2000

OFFICE AND HOUSING, PARISER PLATZ 6A (Bernhard Winking and Martin Froh)
This proposal incorporates the solution adopted by other buildings on Potsdamer Platz to the problem of admitting natural light and air into a deep, narrow site: a glazed atrium with accommodation located along its edges.

Unlike the others, this building has two façades: one on to Pariser Platz and a longer one on to Ebertstraße, each with a two-storey-high passage leading to the inner courtyard. Thus, it will be possible to leave and enter Pariser Platz via this most public of buildings; the lower floors contain shops and cafés to take advantage of the location.

The squarish tower in the corner duplicates the proportions and size of the original prewar building, but the entire stone-clad façade contains no decoration other than a few balconies.

Various architects 1997–2000

Wrapped Reichstag

The Reichstag, the most powerful symbol of twentieth-century Germany, has survived arson, aerial bombing, storming by Russian troops and years of neglect.

Although its exterior was finally restored to some semblance of order (albeit minus the cupola) and its interior redesigned to accommodate congresses and special sittings of the preunification West German government, it remained an empty shell filled with memories in a forgotten corner of the divided city.

The artists Christo and Jeanne Claude first proposed wrapping the Reichstag in 1971. Since then there has been an endless debate as to the project's symbolic meaning. This became academic as the events of 9 November 1989 unfolded. With the vote to move the seat of the government from Bonn to Berlin, the debate on wrapping the Reichstag was once again taken up. The decision to award Norman Foster the contract for converting the Reichstag created a perfect window of opportunity for the project: just before Foster's work began. The wrapping would now be an even more symbolic gesture, marking the transition of Germany from a divided into a reunited country. In a dramatic debate, televised nationwide, the majority of members of parliament voted, despite the objections of Chancellor Kohl, for the wrapped Reichstag project.

A high-strength synthetic woven fabric and Dacron rope were used to wrap the Reichstag for a two-week period at the end of June 1995. Attachment points for the fabric and the ropes employed expanding columns that permitted installation and removal without damaging the building. Specially fabricated cage-like structures protected vulnerable statues and ornaments.

The work was carried out in three phases. The first phase involved all off-site work, including the cutting and sewing of fabric panels. In the

The Wall

Christo and Jeanne Claude 1995

Christo and Jeanne Claude 1995

second phase, the attachment columns and protective cages were installed and the folded fabric panels positioned on the roof. The final phase involved unfurling the fabric and securing it. On-site work was scheduled to take approximately six days. After 14 days, the installation was removed and the materials sold or recycled.

As with all of Christo's works, the project was entirely financed through the sale of preparatory studies, drawings, collages, scale models, early works and original lithographs.

The effect the project had on Berlin was incredible. This work of art was magnetic. Although a circus-like atmosphere almost threatened to turn the work into a backdrop for events occuring around it, in the end the strength, power and sheer beauty of the realised idea won out. Very seldom has a work of art so moved an entire city.

I applaud the decision of the German Bundestag to allow this project to go ahead. You can only imagine the debate in Washington or London over a similar proposal. The German parliament has displayed exceptional courage and maturity.

ADDRESS Platz der Republik, Berlin-Tiergarten [P–11]
COST approximately £10 million
U-BAHN Unter den Linden
S-BAHN Lehrter Stadtbahnhof
BUS 100
ACCESS site open

The Wall

Christo and Jeanne Claude 1995

Christo and Jeanne Claude 1995

Reichstag conversion

Berlin has a sad tradition of organising grand architectural competitions with megalomaniac programmes, announcing winners and then organising a new competition some years later for the same site. A case in point is Aldo Rossi's German Historical Museum. With an exhibition space equivalent to seven football pitches, it would have required the loan of almost the entire collections of Germany's museums to fill it.

A similar situation arose during the first competition for the Reichstag. Sir Norman Foster, Santiago Calatrava and de Bruijn all shared the first prize. Then the realities of cost and size sunk in, and political interference started. Foster won a second competition, with a greatly reduced programme. Gone are the slender columns and the translucent roof; what is left is little more than an internal reorganisation.

The great debate centres on the cupola: should it be built as per the original, as a modern drum, or as a nondescript blob? The parliamentary building commission rejected Foster's preferred glass cylinder, as well as the restoration of the original (favoured by Chancellor Kohl). Instead, they opted for an egg-shaped compromise proposed by the architect.

This cupola will be accessible to the public, with a restaurant at its base and a viewing platform near the top. At the same time, it will deliver natural daylight and ventilation to the debating chamber below.

An additional controversy has erupted over the Cyrillic inscriptions left on the stone walls by Russian soldiers in 1945. Many argue for their retention and integration into the new interior design, as documentation of a historical event and as a reminder to future politicians. Others desire the exorcism of all ghosts and spirits which haunt the building, arguing for a new beginning. Foster finds himself in an unenviable position, caught in the crossfire from all sides.

This building touches the heart and soul of the West Germans and West

The Wall

Sir Norman Foster and Partners

Sir Norman Foster and Partners

Berliners. The Easterners are more interested in the fate of the Palast der Republik. It is a tribute to Foster's skill and determination that anything of architectural integrity can still come out of this project.

ADDRESS Platz der Republik, Berlin-Tiergarten [P–10]
COST DM 600 million
S-BAHN Lehrter Stadtbahnhof
U-BAHN Unter den Linden
BUS 100
ACCESS limited

Sir Norman Foster and Partners

Sir Norman Foster and Partners

Victims' Memorial

To the north of the Reichstag, on the other side of the River Spree, a group of artists has created a very simple, solemn and thought-provoking memorial to the victims of the Berlin Wall.

The death strip was defined here by the water's edge to the west and the inner Wall to the east. On to the individual interconnecting, precast reinforced-concrete slabs of the Wall are painted the yearly totals of those who lost their lives trying to escape. Put simply, this is a macabre score-board documenting the tallies of the SED regime.

Unfortunately, this unofficial, spontaneous work will soon be destroyed by the building of offices for the federal government.

If you had any doubts as to the pure evil of a system which had to erect a Wall to keep its own citizens in and which would shoot dead those who tried to leave, go to this place. Few other memorials are so brutally honest.

ADDRESS Schiffbauerdamm, Berlin-Mitte [P–11]
U-BAHN Friedrichstraße
S-BAHN Lehrter Stadtbahnhof, Friedrichstraße
BUS 100
ACCESS open

The Wall

Unknown artists 1990

Unknown artists 1990

Hamburger Bahnhof

Built in 1847, this small train station quickly bcame outdated and was converted, first into offices, then into a transport museum.

After the war, although physically located in West Berlin, it remained the property of the East German State Railways. It was left empty until 1987 when the city of West Berlin took it over and used it as a space for temporary exhibitions.

The current project involves the conversion of the existing structure, including the main train hall, in close co-operation with the historical preservation authorities. In addition, a new exhibition wing has been constructed parallel to the main hall. Both serve as exhibition space for the magnificent collection of modern art loaned to the city by a private developer. A third wing is planned, but the current budget does not allow for its construction.

The interiors are white and simple, creating an unobtrusive background for the works of art. The initial reaction of the public to the art and building has been overwhelming. The architect must be commended for his skill and restraint.

ADDRESS Invalidenstraße, Berlin-Moabit [P–11]
CLIENT Senatsverwaltung für Bauen, Wohnen und Verkehr
COST approximately DM 100 million
S-BAHN Lehrter Stadtbahnhof
BUS 245, 340
ACCESS open

The Wall

Professor Josef P Kleihues

Professor Josef P Kleihues

Tränenpalast

This is where visitors to East Berlin, as well as old-age pensioners, were processed before being allowed to travel to West Berlin.

It is called the Tränenpalast (palace of tears) for here families would say their goodbyes to mothers, fathers, sisters, brothers, aunts, uncles, grandparents and friends who lived on the other side of the Wall. It was here that the pain caused by the division of the city was most openly expressed.

Once inside, a series of booths and intimidating officials awaited you. Strip searches and other chicanery – as well as a long wait – were routine.

The 'palace' has today been converted into a multiple-use theatre containing a stage, cinema screen and enough loudspeakers to hold discos and rock concerts. Certain elements of the old control apparatus have been creatively reworked into the new: the currency exchange is now a bar and the security monitors a video bank.

The majority of today's visitors never experienced the pain, the fear, and the anger that were once prevalent in this building. It is wonderful that smiles, laughter and joy now pervade it.

ADDRESS s-Bahnhof Friedrichstraße,
Berlin-Mitte [Q–10/11]
U-BAHN Friedrichstraße
s-BAHN Friedrichstraße
ACCESS open to ticket holders

The Wall

1993

The Wall

Boxing arena – Max Schmelling Halle

An international competition was held for a boxing and judo complex as part of Berlin's bid for the 2000 Olympic Games. A group of young German architects won first prize and despite the games being awarded to Sydney the project has been built. The programme includes not only a boxing arena holding 7000 spectators but also a large divisible gymnasium to be used by clubs, schools and the general public. A restaurant, boxing centre, dance schools and a youth club are also located within the building.

The whole complex is built 20 metres deep into a hill of rubble left over from the war. Emerging only 2 metres out of the ground, it integrates with the existing landscape. It appears as an extension of the adjacent Mauerpark rather than a colossus located in the middle of a field. The roof over the wings is grass-covered while a large glass cutout in the main arena roof provides natural light.

This project continues the trend of environmentally friendly sports facilities developed for the winter Olympics at Lillehammer and elsewhere, and proves that such a concept can also be applied successfully in an inner-city area.

ADDRESS Cantianstraße 24, Berlin-Prenzlauer Berg [R–13]
STRUCTURAL ENGINEER Ingenieursozietät BGS
COST DM 200 million
SIZE 25,000 square metres net, 45,000 square metres gross
U-BAHN Eberswalder Straße
S-BAHN Schönhauser Allee
TRAM 13, 20, 50, 53
ACCESS open during events

The Wall

Joppien und Joppien 1996

Joppien und Joppien 1996

S-Bahn Station, Bornholmer Straße

The original s-Bahn station that was built in 1935 to the designs of Richard Brandemann fell victim to the Berlin Wall. On the west side of the bridge was a checkpoint and the railway tracks found themselves running through the middle of the death strip. Although some trains continued to run, none stopped. The station fell into disuse and disrepair.

In 1990, as part of an extensive repair and expansion programme designed to reunite the city, Bornholmer station resumed its role as a key interchange between several s-Bahn lines.

Heavy traffic on the bridge linking East and West Berlin made it almost impossible to cross the road to get to the existing station. A new station was built on the north side which connects with the existing station on the south side under the bridge.

The new structure uses a lightweight steel-skeleton system, clad in blue-grey, corrugated-aluminium panels. Natural daylight floods into the enclosed connecting corridors through the use of glass blocks and large areas of glazing with mullions reflecting the 1930s theme.

Combined with the restored original, this new station is a well-designed, well-detailed addition to the rich tradition of railway architecture in Berlin.

ADDRESS Bösebrücke, Berlin-Pankow [Q–14]
CLIENT Land Berlin, Deutsche Reichsbahn
COST DM 30 million
U-BAHN Bornholmer Straße
TRAM 23, 24, 52
ACCESS open

The Wall

Dörr, Ludolf, Wimmer 1993

Dörr, Ludolf, Wimmer 1993

Mitte

Maritim Hotel

Hidden behind the newly added plates of granite and glass is the original 1977 reinforced-concrete core of the Hotel Metropol. The architects have given this former DDR showpiece a 'Western' appearance and have totally remodelled the interior to provide conference rooms, offices and shops.

The only entirely new structure is that overlooking Friedrichstraße. This re-establishes the street line that had not been observed by the existing hotel.

This type of cosmetic surgery is not only confined to this hotel, it can be seen throughout the eastern part of the city. It remains to be seen how much time has to pass before another facelift is due.

ADDRESS Friedrichstraße corner Mittelstraße, 10117 Berlin-Mitte [Q–10]
CLIENT Deutsche Interhotels
U-BAHN Friedrichstraße
S-BAHN Friedrichstraße
BUS 100
ACCESS open

Mitte

Nettbaum + Partner 1995

Nettbaum + Partner 1995

Parliamentary offices

To house the enormous government bureaucracy that is scheduled to move to Berlin, many buildings of the previous East German regime are currently being refurbished and reclad to Western standards.

This particular building, formerly the DDR Ministry for Foreign and Inter-German Trade, is being converted to house offices for members of parliament and their secretaries. Once the building had been stripped down to its structural core, an extra floor was added to continue the eaves line of its neighbours. The new façade of stone and glass reflects the current fashion for façades of holes (*Lochfassaden*).

A similar exercise has been carried out by Gehrmann Consult GmbH at Unter den Linden 69–73. The former DDR Ministry for Education (built in 1964) was converted in 1996 and now houses the Federal Ministry for Buildings and City Planning. This too follows the four new commandments of building in central Berlin: *Lochfassade*; an adherence to the 22-metre eaves line; stone cladding; and building to the street edge with no setbacks or wild forms. The resulting buildings, however, only go to illustrate just how boring this can be.

ADDRESS Unter den Linden 44–60, Berlin-Mitte [P–10]
COST DM 121 million
SIZE 33,700 square metres
S-BAHN Unter den Linden
BUS 100, 348
ACCESS none

Mitte

Alexander Kolbe – Freie Architekten 1997

Alexander Kolbe – Freie Architekten 1997

Mitte

Haus-Pietzsch

On a narrow corner site, the architect has designed an ingenious floor plan to overcome the inherent problems of natural light and internal circulation. Rather than being centrally located, the main entrance has been shifted to the edge of the neighbouring fire wall. This has freed up a shaft of space that runs along its entire length and height, creating a narrow atrium as the internal circulation system. The office space is uniquely arranged so that the rear zones can be accessed only through the front zones which connect to the circulation galleries. This arrangement allows for natural light to penetrate the interior offices via the atrium while keeping circulation space to a minimum.

The fire wall of the atrium is painted white and doubles as a museum wall for the art collection of the owners. Various exhibitions are planned which will allow the atrium to function as a public space.

The exterior façade is clearly divided between base, middle and roof, each with its respective functions (restaurants, offices and penthouses).

The street lines and building edges have been re-established and the building sits comfortably on its site. It is one of the few genuine successes of recent years.

ADDRESS Unter den Linden 42, Berlin-Mitte [P–10]
CLIENT Unter den Linden 42 GbR
SIZE 3300 square metres (offices); 800 square metres (shops)
U-BAHN Friedrichstraße
S-BAHN Unter den Linden
BUS 100, 147
ACCESS open

Mitte

Jürgen Sawade 1995

Jürgen Sawade 1995

Lindencorso

On this, the most important site in Berlin, the positive and negative results of this city's architectural debate over critical reconstruction can be clearly seen.

The urban planning side of this debate has been successfully implemented. The building restores the street edge (the 1960s structure had been set back from Unter den Linden) and respects the traditional 22-metre eaves line. As part of the restoration of the Friedrichstraße to its historical width, the new building has incorporated an arcade along its side. The arcade contains the main entrance into a three-level shopping gallery. In addition to the shops, the building includes a German-French business and cultural institute, as well as a trade and studies centre.

While it is possible to 'critically reconstruct' city blocks, urban spaces and building programmes, this building shows that it is not possible to transplant this concept on to façades. The use of stone, a grid of holes, and precast-concrete details are not enough to recreate a sense of the lost heritage. Instead, it leads to a poor imitation of Albert Speer's Germania.

West Berlin architects universally condemned the nearby Grand Hotel when it was opened in the late 1980s as a laughable example of East German architecture, but at least it was honest about itself.

ADDRESS Unter den Linden corner, Friedrichstraße, Berlin-Mitte [Q–10]
CLIENT Lindencorso Grundstücksgesellschaft mbH Berlin
SIZE 47,000 square metres gross
COST DM 150 million
U-BAHN Friedrichstraße, Französische Straße
BUS 100, 147
ACCESS open

Mitte

Christoph Mäckler 1996

Christoph Mäckler 1996

Friedrichstadt was laid out in 1688. Over the years the smaller original buildings were added to or replaced with larger structures and the area changed from being mainly residential with a few small businesses until by 1945 it was predominantly commercial.

Heavily damaged during the war, only four of the buildings in this block survived. In his masterplan, Josef P Kleihues used these buildings as a starting point for the rebuilding. Their position broke the block into smaller entities which were then distributed among four architects to achieve variety and a breakdown in scale. The 22-metre eaves line, stepped-back roof storeys and the building lines were the main guidelines. Also common to all is the large garden courtyard in the centre of the block.

The idea of critical reconstruction in terms of city planning is a continuation of the work of the IBA (of which Kleihues was director). However, critical reconstruction when applied to façades has unleashed an intense debate. Unfortunately, the resulting mixture of real and historicist modernism is not up to the quality of the city planning.

ADDRESS Friedrichstraße, Charlottenstraße, Behrenstraße, Französische Straße, Berlin-Mitte [Q–10]
CLIENT Hines Grundstücksentwicklungs GmbH
ARCHITECTS Max Dudler (housing, Behrenstraße); Professor Josef P Kleihues (hotel, Charlottenstraße); Hans Kollhoff (offices, Friedrichstraße); Jürgen Sawade (offices, Französische Straße)
SIZE hotel 16,500 square metres; offices 22,000 square metres; housing 8000 square metres; commercial space 3500 square
U-BAHN Stadtmitte, Französische Straße
BUS 147
ACCESS limited

Mitte

Professor Josef P Kleihues et al 1996

Professor Josef P Kleihues et al 1996

Friedrichstadt-Passage

The name of the project is misleading. It is named after the underground multilevel shopping arcade linking blocks 205, 206 and 207. What the visitor does see are three huge commercial developments which have three very different architectural approaches to promoting the reinstatement of Friedrichstraße as Berlin's foremost shopping and entertainment street.

The best-known of the three is Jean Nouvel's Galeries Lafayettes, a glass whirlwind containing shops, restaurants, offices and cabaret, as well as the eponymous department store. The building respects the 22-metre eaves height and building lines of its surviving neighbours, and wraps itself around the corner, pushing the main entrance of the department store into the Friedrichstraße, emphasising the street's importance. From there one enters the central shopping space which has a naturally lit conical atrium extending through the roof and penetrating down into the levels below ground. This void deceives the visitor into thinking that the store is larger than it is, for the amount of sales area is, in comparison, quite small. The atrium also heightens the sense of excitement and dynamism, becoming at the same time a focus of relaxation for tired shoppers.

The Friedrichstraße needed a department store that could compete with Ka De We in former West Berlin, and Nouvel has provided it.

The second development, the middle block, is an attempt to reinterpret 1920s art deco and Berlin's tradition of façadal appendages. Here, Henry Cobb of Pei, Cobb Freed + Partner has broken the long façades into a series of almost undulating projections, which can only be seen from the viewpoint of the passerby. The building is the most Berlinesque within the ensemble. It appears massive, heavy and overpowering. However, the effect is reversed at night when the light emanating from within forms an almost whimsical pattern, reminiscent of exterior cinema lighting. The interior atrium is overwhelming. The flooring material and patterns

Mitte

Various architects 1996

Various architects 1996

exude luxury. For many architects, it is overdone. For the everyday shopper, it is a feast for the eye. Even the glazing of the atrium's roof is broken into crystalline forms which add to the visual attraction. However, as a whole, the space is nervous rather than confident.

The third and most restrained development is that from O M Ungers. Taking up the entire block, the building is one huge eight-storey structure, set back from the street. Attached are six-storey projecting cubes which re-establish the street edge and the 22-metre eaves height relationship. The spaces between the cubes are the entrances to the various cores and passages. Through the use of the projecting cubes, the light colour of the sandstone cladding, and repetition of his trademark squares, Ungers has been able to reduce the massiveness to an acceptable level. The building forms a quiet background for the historical buildings of the Gendarmenmarkt (Platz der Akademie).

Whether the actual passage linking all three blocks will be successful is in doubt. There is no hint of it from the street; the passerby must already know that it exists. The life that is so needed on the Friedrichstraße is actually removed and placed deep inside the buildings, defeating one of the primary goals of the city-planning concept.

ADDRESS Friedrichstraße between Französische Straße and Mohrenstraße, Berlin-Mitte [Q–10]
COST DM 100 million (block 206); DM 150 million (block 207)
SIZE 52,000 square metres net (block 205); 44,500 square metres net (block 206); 40,000 square metres (block 207)
U-BAHN Stadtmitte, Französische Straße
BUS 147
ACCESS shopping hours

Mitte

Various architects 1996

Mitte

Various architects 1996

Kontorhaus Mitte

Prior to 1989, the East German government had plans to redevelop the eastern half of block 209. The block itself had been heavily damaged during the war – in fact only one original prewar building remained.

The post-Wall planning for this site was headed by Josef P Kleihues. Again it invoked the concept of critical reconstruction (see page 228): the re-establishment of street and building lines, as well as 22-metre eaves heights, and the generous use of stone cladding on the façades with holes punched in as fenestration.

What is different here is the circulation system. Galleries are composed around an interior square atrium, with extensions reaching out to the street containing the vertical circulation. This system expresses itself as an element in its own right. It both subdivides the block into individual plots and encompasses the one remaining structure.

Each plot was assigned to a different architect in order to achieve variety in the treatment of the individual façades. The interior courtyard is spanned by a large glazed roof that ties all the structures together into one ensemble.

ADDRESS Friedrichstraße 185–190, Berlin-Mitte [Q–10]
CLIENT Argenta Int.
ARCHITECTS Klaus Theo Brenner (Friedrichstraße corner Kronenstraße); Professor Josef P Kleihues (Friedrichstraße); Vittorio Lampugnani (Mohrenstraße); Walther Stepp (Friedrichstraße corner with Mohrenstraße)
SIZE 33,500 square metres gross
U-BAHN Friedrichstraße, Stadtmitte
BUS 147, 257
ACCESS open

Mitte

Various architects 1996

Various architects 1996

Atrium

The L-shaped site for this development was located in a half-destroyed block, with buildings remaining on its eastern half and an isolated free-standing structure in the northwest corner. In order to maximise the amount of office space, two atriums were created in the middle of each leg of the L in order to ensure natural daylight. A third atrium was created by indenting slightly one leg of the L to allow light and air to the corner building. The atriums are not located on the ground floor; instead, a mezzanine level has been created which can be reached only by escalator after passing the guard's desk. Shops are provided along the Leipziger Straße at street level under a two-storey arcade, thus re-establishing a forgotten Berlin tradition.

A tower marks the corner of Leipziger Straße and Friedrichstraße and acts as a pendant to the existing corner building in the Friedrichstraße.

The treatment of the façade breaks with the current vogue for vertical holes punched in a flat plane of stone. Instead, the structural grid is exposed and the large horizontal areas between the columns are fully glazed. The main debate will centre around the façade, comparing it with those of its neighbours who practise 'critical reconstruction'.

ADDRESS Friedrichstraße 59–60, Leipziger Straße 101–102 [Q–10]
CLIENT Grundstücks-Kommanditgesellschaft Küllmann & Co.
SIZE 32,000 square metres gross
U-BAHN Stadtmitte
BUS 147
ACCESS open

Mitte

von Gerkan, Marg und Partner 1996

von Gerkan, Marg und Partner 1996

Am Gendarmenmarkt

Designed not to be noticed, this ensemble of three office buildings takes banality to a higher level than achieved elsewhere under the guise of critical reconstruction.

Given that it is hard to compete with Karl Friedrich Schinkel's masterpiece (the Schauspielhaus) and the two churches across the street, the architects apparently decided to play background music. It is better not to offend anybody than to please a few.

In contrast, the prefabricated structures erected during the last days of the DDR (especially those along Markgrafenstraße between Französische Straße and Gendarmenstraße) look extremely detailed and refined, considering the restrictions the architects were working under.

ADDRESS Taubenstraße, Markgrafenstraße, Mohrenstraße, Berlin-Mitte [Q–10]
ARCHITECTS Professor Josef P Kleihues (Markgrafenstraße 34); Max Dudler (Markgrafenstraße 35); Hilmer und Sattler (Markgrafenstraße 36)
SIZE total 17,000 square metres gross
U-BAHN Stadtmitte, Hausvogteiplatz
BUS 147
ACCESS open

Mitte

Various architects 1997

Various architects 1997

Deutsche Bank

Unfortunately, little information about this interesting project could be obtained.

It appears that in order to restore the bank to its original condition a later roof storey, overlooking the Unter den Linden, is being removed from the corner building. However, two new roof storeys are being added to the back along the Charlottenstraße side. What catches the eye is the glazed wall protruding approximately a metre in front of the Charlottenstraße façade. Elegantly executed, it can only be guessed that this provides the necessary sound insulation for the offices behind, as well as integrating the new roof storeys architecturally.

The interior halls are being restored and some are being expanded. If the reputation of the Deutsche Bank is anything to go by, the finishes will be exquisite.

ADDRESS Unter den Linden 13–15, Berlin-Mitte [Q–10]
CLIENT Debeko Immobilien GmbH & Co.
U-BAHN Französische Straße
BUS 100, 348
ACCESS not confirmed

Mitte

Novotny Mähner & Assoziierte Architekten 1997

Novotny Mähner & Assozierte Architekten 1997

Underground library

This is a wonderfully conceived and executed project that few people know about or even notice.

To mark the location of the Nazis' bookburning of 10 May 1933, a competition was held for the design of a memorial that would not only document the event, but also serve as a warning for future generations. Micha Ullman, an Israeli artist, proposed the installation of a space 7 x 7 x 5 metres high, located entirely underground in the middle of Bebelplatz. The room is an imaginary library containing empty white shelves on which the 20,000 lost books could have been housed. Visitors can only see into the space through a 1.2 x 1.2-metre glass plate.

During the day, the installation is not visible from the street, but at night a beam of light streams out through the glass plate, announcing both its presence and its message. The idea of locating this library underground also solved the problem of building a three-dimensional intervention on the historic Bebelplatz.

The size of the project has proved that any monument, whatever the magnitude of the event, does not itself have to be monumental in scale. It is the idea represented and communicated by the memorial that is important, not the monument.

ADDRESS Bebelplatz, Unter den Linden, Berlin-Mitte [Q–10]
U-BAHN Hausvogteiplatz
BUS 100
ACCESS open

Mitte

Micha Ullman (artist) and Andreas Zerr (architect) 1996

Micha Ullman (artist) and Andreas Zerr (architect) 1996

Schloß Mirror and Palast der Republik

In 1443, the original city palace of the ruling Hohenzollern family was built here. Renaissance and baroque additions eventually created a larger complex, strategically placed at the end of the Unter den Linden. The architect Karl Friedrich Schinkel based his concept for his nearby buildings on this urban configuration. The palace and its cupola became the centre of Berlin. Heavily damaged during the street fighting of 1919, the palace's portal was the stage on which Karl Liebkneck proclaimed the first German Socialist Republic.

On ideological grounds, the entire Schloß was demolished in 1950, leaving only the portal. This was moved across the street and incorporated into the façade of the Staatsratgebäude where the leaders of communist East Germany had their offices.

In its place, the Palast der Republik was erected in 1976. Seen today as a vacant relic of a collapsed system, it neither respects the historical termination of Unter den Linden nor the axial relationship to the Berliner Dom or Schinkel's Altes Museum. Its larger paved 'platz' was most often used as a car park, but on state occasions it was a place for mass assembly. The building contained the parliamentary chamber of the GDR, as well as various meeting rooms, 13 restaurants and a 5000-seat multi-use hall.

With no parliament to house (the West Germans will move back into the Reichstag, which in fact does not have a very good democratic record), and an alleged asbestos problem – although recent studies show that it could be cleaned up within a reasonable budget – the building stands empty.

During 1994, a private group organised an exhibition documenting the Kaiser's original palace. As part of this, a gigantic scaffold was erected in the platz and a full-size painted replica of the façade was hung from it. Using a mirror mounted on the façade of the existing structure, it was

Mitte

Mitte

Förderverein Berliner Stadtschloß eV 1993–94

possible to project an image of its correct historical length when seen from the bridge.

A vital piece was missing, however – the cupola at the western end. In spite of this, the image still looked impressive. If the dome could have been projected it would have been an imposing, almost convincing, argument for restoration. Without it, many consider the project not worth the expense.

A recent competition was held in the area. The first prize proposed building a modern structure that would be exactly the same size as the original, minus the cupola.

The debate will rage on between those who want to rebuild historically and those who argue that modernism can also create great architecture on a historic site. What will remain, though, is the memory of the mirror that showed us an image lost.

ADDRESS Unter den Linden, Berlin-Mitte [R–10]
BUS 100, 157
S-BAHN Alexanderplatz
U-BAHN Alexanderplatz

Mitte

Förderverein Berliner Stadtschloß eV 1993–94

Förderverein Berliner Stadtschloß eV 1993–94

Hackesche Höfe

This labyrinth of buildings and courtyards is one of the best remaining examples of its type. Offices are situated along the street edge while small-scale workshops are in the courtyards; housing is above and to the rear. This world in miniature – rich and poor, housing and commerce, all crammed in side by side and on top of each other – was what prewar Berlin, the Berlin of stone, was all about, for all its good and evil.

This mixed-use held sway beyond 1989, although the buildings had deteriorated. A sense of romantic decay had in fact added to its charm. After the collapse of the DDR, a battle raged over property rights and design proposals. In the end, the investor had to accede to the users as well as to the authorities responsible for historic preservation. The compromises ensured a mix of cultural activities along with renovated housing and viable office space. The results are impressive. The life of the courtyards attracts businesses to the office space, in turn generating more business for the cafés, cabaret, shops and galleries in the courtyards.

Of architectural note are the fine modern interiors of the Aedes East Gallery and Café, both by the Dutch architect Ben van Berkel. Long established as the centre of West Berlin's architectural scene, Aedes, through its expansion, along with the recently established DAZ and the relocated Architektenkammer, has now shifted architectural society to the East, into the eye of the building hurricane currently sweeping through the city.

ADDRESS Rosenthaler Straße, Berlin-Mitte [R–11]
CLIENT Roland Ernst
U-BAHN Weinmeister Straße
S-BAHN Hackescher Markt
TRAM 1, 2, 3, 4, 5, 13, 53
ACCESS open

Ben van Berkel (Aedes) 1996

Mitte

Neue Synagogue

According to the laws of the time, no non-Protestant place of worship could be a detached structure; it had to be part of the building block. Completed in 1866 by Friedrich August Stüler, this synagogue was the largest and most lavish in the city. Built in a Moorish style, it attracted great interest for its ingenious use of iron and glass. Set on fire during Kristallnacht in 1938 and further damaged by air raids in 1943, it remained a ruin until 1989 when reconstruction started.

The rebuilt synagogue symbolises the slow rebirth of Berlin's Jewish community. Immigration from Eastern Europe during the 1980s has led to the re-establishment of a Jewish school as well as other organisations (see page 78).

This building, like Daniel Libeskind's Jewish Museum (see page 98), powerfully documents the influence that the Jewish community once had on all aspects of life and culture in Berlin, and how much has been lost and is still missing.

After all this time and all that has happened, it is obscene that it is necessary to station police around the building to protect it from attack by right-wing extremists.

ADDRESS Oranienburger Straße 30, Berlin-Mitte [Q–11]
S-BAHN Oranienburger Straße
U-BAHN Oranienburger Tor
TRAM 1, 13, 24
ACCESS visible from street

Mitte

Edward Knoblauch 1993

Tacheles

Built in 1909 as a department store, Tacheles had a passage linking the Oranienburger Straße with the Friedrichstraße. Its entire structural system, including one of Europe's largest ribbed cupolas, is of reinforced concrete. As well as shops, it has housed, at various times, cinemas, offices, the ss land registry office, French prisoners of war, East German schools of art and economics and a unit of the National Volksarmee.

Severely damaged during the war, it remained in use until the early 1980s when parts of it along the Friedrichstraße were demolished. Artists and squatters occupied the ruin shortly after the East German regime fell from power in 1990. Agreement was reached with the local authority to list the building and to carry out emergency repairs.

Within the labyrinth of rooms and spaces, more than 100 artists and musicians now live and work. On the upper floor are workshops and studios, in the basement are performance areas. The energy released at the beginning was incredible; Tacheles became a symbol for adventure and experimentation. But a sense of disappointment has crept in as the original members have departed. The second generation is now locked in battle with a developer over the ground behind the buildings. As part of a carefully thought-out urban design proposal this space would become the central focus of the block's development, a public forum for performances and art. The proposed buildings are divided into small plots, to be sold off to individual owners, leading to variety and differentiation. It remains to be seen what the outcome will be.

ADDRESS Oranienburger Straße, Berlin-Mitte [Q–11]
S-BAHN Oranienburger Straße
TRAM 1, 13, 24
ACCESS open

Mitte

Platz vor dem Neuen Tor

Located near the former Checkpoint Invalidenstraße, this district, badly damaged in the war, became almost a no-go area for both Easterners and Westerners. This project attempts to repair and heal the wounds of the last 50 years and to restore an urban identity. The triangular block bounded by Invalidenstraße, Hessische Straße and Hannoverische Straße still contains building remnants that survived the war. Kleihues has proposed repairing the block by re-establishing the street and building lines, respecting the heights of the existing buildings and breaking up the programme into identifiable elements.

An office building occupies the apex of the triangle, with two apartment blocks located on the southwest corner, and a triangular block along the southeast containing apartments with unconventional floor plans. The form of this last building is determined not only by the block geometry, but also by its incorporation of the remaining fragments of an old city wall. A break between the building and that on the corner allows the preservation of a large tree which managed to grow in the rubble. At the southern end twin gate houses will be reinstated which will regenerate the proper scale of the platz and provide an edge and an identity.

The architect has identified an important urban space that during the course of history had almost been forgotten. It is through such thoughtful projects that Berliners are reminded of how much they have lost.

ADDRESS Platz vor dem Neuen Tor, Berlin-Mitte [P–11]
CLIENT Bayerischer Hausbau
U-BAHN Zinno-Witzer-Straße
S-BAHN Lehrter Stadtbahnhof
BUS 245, 340
ACCESS open

Mitte

Professor Josef P Kleihues 1997

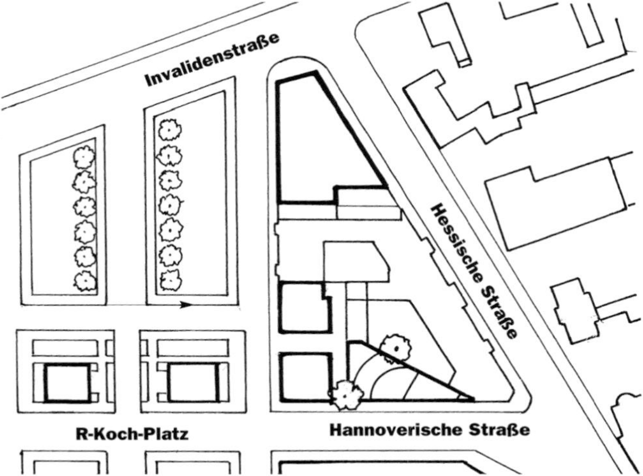

Invalidenstraße

Platz vor dem Neuen Tor

Hessische Straße

R-Koch-Platz

Hannoverische Straße

Mitte

Professor Josef P Kleihues 1997

Ostkreuz to Adlershof

Offices at Ostkreuz

Squeezed within the junction of four major s-Bahn stations, this dense office complex is perfectly suited to its location.

It is divided into three distinct zones: the first is an impressive renovated red-brick office building; the second is a grid of eight-storey offices arranged around a series of planted courtyards; and the third is a 13-storey aluminium and glass arc that reflects the curve of the neighbouring s-Bahn.

The detailing is well executed and the colours and materials of the central blocks make a successful transition between the existing brick building and the new architecture.

Unlike so many other offices complexes, this one makes sense due to its location and accessibility by public transport.

Ostkreuz to Adlershof

ADDRESS Schreiberhauer Straße/Kaskelstraße, Berlin-Lichtenberg [v–9]
CLIENT GbR Dienstleistungszentrum Ostkreuz
S-BAHN Ostkreuz, Nöldnerplatz, Frankfurter Allee
BUS 240
ACCESS open

J S K Perkins + Will 1996

J S K Perkins + Will 1996

BESSY II

Located partly on the first airfield for powered flight in Germany, this area is now being developed as a major complex for scientific research, media technology and associated businesses. Even before the Wall came down, the buildings served as one of East Germany's main scientific research centres and was the home of DDR television.

Many projects are already under construction, including the Photonik Innovation Centre by Sauerbruch and Hutten, as well as the electron storage ring BESSY II.

The core building of BESSY II consists of a circular reinforced-concrete structure, clad in metal panels.

At the client's request, the architects were not able to supply more information concerning this unique building at this time. However, the Exhibition and Information Centre will be giving out any available news as work progresses.

ADDRESS Magnusstraße, Berlin-Adlershof [Y–3]
Exhibition and Information Centre, Rudower Chaussee 3,
Berlin-Adlershof
S-BAHN Adlershof
BUS 260
Access Monday to Friday 10.00–16.00; telephone 670 44 701

Brenner + Partners 1996

Ostkreuz to Adlershof

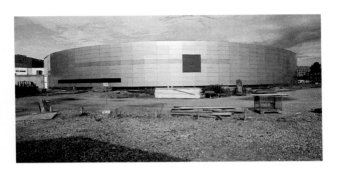

Brenner + Partners 1996

Prenzlauer Berg to Hellersdorf

Quasar

The Frankfurter Allee is the main thoroughfare leading into the historic core of East Berlin. Shortly before reaching the buildings of the 'Stalin Allee', an incredible composition of glass, steel and black granite meets your eye. Shin Takamatsu and Gabriel E Lahyani have created a *tour de force* to house a bank and offices.

Contrary to initial impressions, this building has its roots thoroughly planted in Berlin's architectural history. The effective use of lighting as a compositional element was demonstrated in the cinema architecture of Rudolf Fränkel and others during the 1930s. This building is 1990s art deco.

The rest of the block re-establishes the edges to the street. Consisting of offices, a hotel, housing and retail units, the interior courtyard acts to unite these divergent usages under a glazed roof. The development is extremely dense and the architecture nondescript.

ADDRESS Frankfurter Allee 69, Berlin-Friedrichshain [v–10]
CLIENT Fundus Fonds Nr 28
COST DM 160 million
SIZE 4000 square metres
U-BAHN Samariter Straße
S-BAHN Frankfurter Allee
ACCESS open

Shin Takamatsu and Gabriel E Lahyani 1994–95

Shin Takamatsu and Gabriel E Lahyani 1994–95

Sportforum

Located deep within a compound containing a bizarre collection of assorted gyms and swimming pools, this remarkable building is becoming well known not only for its architecture, but also for its programmatic innovation.

The building is divided architecturally into two distinct areas: the first is a one-storey metal-clad container housing service areas, offices and changing rooms; the second comprises a glass-and-steel-enclosed gymnasium and associated sports areas linked together by an undulating, laminated timber-braced roof.

Its greatest innovation lies in the location of the various boxes and cages for javelin, discus, shotput and hammerthrow under the undulating roof. These glass-enclosed facilities have large doors opening out on to the adjoining athletic fields so that both training and official events can take place regardless of the weather.

Each of the disciplines required a different enclosure, depending upon the athletes' movement and that of their equipment through space. The architects have achieved a delightful play of forms which, through the extension of the undulating roof, they have succeeded in uniting into a visible whole.

ADDRESS Sportforum Berlin, Weißenseer Weg 51–55, Berlin-Weissensee [v–12]
CLIENT OSB Sportstättenbauten GmbH
COST DM 18 million
S-BAHN Landsberger Allee
TRAM 5, 15, 23
ACCESS open

CFB-IPRO Berlin 1995

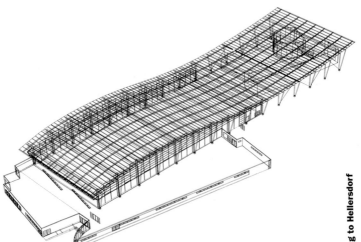

Prenzlauer Berg to Hellersdorf

CFB-IPRO Berlin 1995

Velodrome/Swimmstadion

The main problem when planning a sports facility is to reconcile the need of major or international events for a large seating capacity with the fact that for most of the time only minor, local events requiring far fewer seats will be taking place. Another major problem for the architect is integrating such a complex into the local community while at the same time accommodating the large number of outsiders who will visit the special events.

Dominique Perrault has successfully united these criteria in his design for the Velodrome and Swimmstadion complex.

Two districts of Berlin are physically divided by a culverted train line. The complex spans this, linking the districts. This simple act also accommodates the arrival of visitors by incorporating the s-Bahn station and the line that links various other sporting facilities in East and West Berlin. Thus, international events such as the Olympics could be held in downtown Berlin without associated traffic jams.

To the north, Perrault has created a platz and located office and commercial space along its edge. To the south, he has proposed additional housing in a typical Berlin-block manner to complete the existing urban pattern.

Between the two is an apple orchard, under which the sports complex is located, the only hint of its presence being the shiny metallic roofs of the two amphitheatres. During the day, the reflective knitted-metal surface gives the impression of water; evening light radiates outwards, creating a magical spectacle.

The orchard has steps built into it so that by raising the roof (using temporary jacks) additional seating can be accommodated for major events. Otherwise, the roof remains level with the surface, providing the capacity required for smaller events.

Prenzlauer Berg to Hellersdorf

Dominique Perrault 1994–96

Dominique Perrault 1994–96

The architect admits that high technology played no role in his building. Simple, normal construction techniques make this clear, rational, elegant complex financially attractive.

ADDRESS Landsberger Allee, Fritz-Riedel-Straße, Berlin-Prenzlauer Berg [U–11]
CLIENT Olympia 2000 Sportstättenbauten GmbH
STRUCTURAL ENGINEER Ove Arup & Partners
S-BAHN Landsberger Allee
ACCESS open during events

Dominique Perrault 1994–96

Dominique Perrault 1994–96

Landsberger Arcade

The Landsberger Allee (formerly Leninallee) is one of the most depressing routes into and out of the city. Generally heavily congested with traffic, the surroundings are rarely noticed and are of little note.

However, with this project Aldo Rossi tries to re-establish the traditional urban block. His concept is based on four towers, each located at a corner, with lower buildings spanning between them. Each of these is broken down further into individual buildings, in order to achieve variety and to restore a sense of scale.

Offices, a hotel, shops and restaurants make up the programme. Due to the proximity of the s-Bahn, the new sports facility and the housing development nearby, it is calculated that this project will form the new centre of a functioning neighbourhood. Whether this succeeds remains to be seen but, architecturally, when completed it will be a significant improvement to the current barren and grey landscape of nondescript concrete blocks.

ADDRESS Landsberger Allee 106, Berlin-Prenzlauer Berg [U–11]
CLIENTS Dr Peter and Isolde Kottmair GbR
SIZE 42,000 square metres
S-BAHN Landsberger Allee
TRAM 5, 6, 7, 8, 15, 27

Aldo Rossi/Götz + Böhm

Aldo Rossi/Götz + Böhm

Housing, Simon Bolivar Straße

This is where the visitor to Berlin can experience over 60 years of social housing theory, all within a few streets. The structure of the area is defined by long housing blocks, each dating from a different decade. 1930s modernism as well as a range of postwar East German designs (including several variations of precast-concrete-panel systems) sit side by side. One can see the continuing 'progress' of the building industry over time, in terms of standardisation, production and aesthetics. Set in this lifeless landscape is this new housing estate with a density far higher than that of its neighbours.

At first, the long white and black housing units by Pudritz and Paul seem overpowering. The treatment of the external façade, when compared with that of its neighbours, is heavy handed and the fenestration in the corners between the main block and the courtyard wings is of a questionable quality. On closer inspection, however, the straightforward detailing and *Lochfassade* (façade of holes) does reflect more closely the tradition of Berlin.

Though Hoppenbrink's units are larger, they have been broken down into four independent villas. The treatment of the eaves gives the roof a whimsical touch compared with those by Pudritz and Paul. This is the extent, however, to which the detailing can be deemed notable.

This estate continues the concept of satellite town development where the residents must drive to work, returning only to sleep.

ADDRESS Simon Bolivar Straße, Berlin-Hohenschönhausen [W–12]
CLIENT Immobilienfonds Ziel 7 GbR
MASTERPLAN Horst Ziel
TRAM 6, 7
ACCESS open

Paul Hoppenbrink and Pudritz und Paul 1994

Paul Hoppenbrink and Pudritz und Paul 1994

Housing, Hansastraße

From sketches to 1:100 scale drawings in just eight weeks; this project is typical of what is happening in the East.

Shortly after the Wall came down, a piece of land suitable for housing was sold off by the Church to raise money for modernising a hospital. With nothing but a flat field to work with and only typical *Plattenbau* (concrete-panel buildings) across the street, the architects tried to give this housing estate some sort of identity and sense of place. A central axis was created for orientation and as an outside space for meetings and events. The housing behind the axis is organised as a series of wings off the main buildings and smaller villas are placed in the courtyards. Overall the project is very effective, except at the estate's boundaries where it is apparent that it lacks a neighbourhood or any kind of urban context.

As it is, this is a pleasant place to live and the flats are well designed with good views to the green spaces. Car parking is carefully allocated and the landscaping, although it will take time to reach maturity, already provides a hint of its eventual quality. The only problem is that this perfect solution to an urban infill site is not located on an urban infill site. It is to be hoped that eventually the 'urban' will spring up around it.

ADDRESS Hansastraße 65–149, Berlin-Weissensee [v–13]
CLIENT Groth + Graalfs
PROJECT LEADER Jorg Fischer
STRUCTURAL ENGINEER Herbert Pape GmbH
COST DM 100 million
SIZE 35,096 square metres net
TRAM 3
BUS 259
ACCESS open

Prenzlauer Berg to Hellersdorf

Fedderson, von Herder und Partner 1994

Fedderson, von Herder und Partner 1994

The Pyramide

Marzahn is synonymous with an East Berlin of soulless factory-made housing, lacking any sense of urban design and infrastructure. At a major intersection, a new office and light-industrial complex has been erected that symbolises this emptiness.

A long, low, curtain-walled block containing service industry accommodation is located along the Rhinstraße, and on the corner a flesh-coloured granite clads two thin office towers with a pyramid-like glass element slicing between them.

This building could be in Houston, or anywhere else. It has no relationship with its surroundings. However, since it had no surroundings to begin with, the architect has decided to make a grand gesture instead.

Prenzlauer Berg to Hellersdorf

ADDRESS Rhinstraße, corner of Landsberger Allee, Berlin-Marzahn [X–12]
CLIENT Fundus Fonds Nr 27
STRUCTURAL ENGINEER Grebner Ingenieure, Dr Ing. Reinhard Mang
COST DM 130 million
BUS 294
TRAM 6, 7, 18, 26
ACCESS open

Regina Schuh with Architekturbüro Tactic 1994–95

Regina Schuh with Architekturbüro Tactic 1994–95

Housing, Ridbacher Straße

An unexpected delight on an unassuming site. The district of Hellersdorf is generally associated with its prefabricated housing blocks and the major project now under construction to build the new district centre. Unknown to many are the small-scale infill projects such as this which have been carried out quietly in the last few years.

Located on a corner, the building contains much needed space for small shops and services on the ground floor with flats above. The building is actually split into two, giving the north building a finely composed and proportioned façade.

The detailing is crisp and clean, and the careful attention given to materials and their surfaces is evident.

Although the building is difficult to get to, if combined with other Hellersdorfer projects (in particular the new centre by Brandt + Böttcher at U-Bahn Hellersdorf) it is well worth a visit.

ADDRESS Ridbacher Straße 1–7, Berlin-Hellersdorf [II E–17]
CLIENT Penz + Pless GbR
COST DM 8.3 million
S-BAHN Mahlsdorf
BUS 195, 198, 197, 199
ACCESS open

Becher + Rottkamp 1995

Becher + Rottkamp 1995

Housing, Wernerstraße

The site consisted of long and narrow strips on each side of the street. The buildings were conceived in their massing and placement as a transition between the huge prefabricated housing complex to the west and the small-scale, scattered houses to the east, north and south.

Those along the north side of Wernerstraße are oriented to the west in order to provide private gardens and to catch the late afternoon sun. Those on the south side are oriented directly south, overlooking the park landscape.

The first building type is semi-detached housing, constructed out of prefabricated timber elements; the second type is more conventional, using blockwork construction. Conceived as a 'city villa', this type contains apartments with units ranging from one and a half to four rooms in size.

The architects have succeeded in creating an identity for this small development on a difficult transitional site. When the planting matures, the units should fit in quite well with their neighbours.

ADDRESS Wernerstraße 6–10 and 26–36 [IID–17]
CLIENT Wohnungsbaugesellschaft Hellersdorf mbH
COST DM 30.8 million
S-BAHN Mahlsdorf
BUS 199
ACCESS open

Casa Nova 1995

Casa Nova 1995

Pankow to Karow

Housing, Kastanienallee

This project is the result of an urban-planning competition in which the four top-placed architects were awarded commissions to design various housing units in compliance with the winning masterplan.

Along the site's edges, two-storey, single-family houses are planned to provide a transition from the typical one-storey house of the neighbourhood to the larger blocks of flats of three or four storeys in the centre of the development. The interior is conceived as two groups of three U-shaped courts containing a mixture of flat types. Separating these two groups is a large triangular public green space which is laid out like a garden and contains a water feature and various other amenities.

Along the main street, small shops are planned at the ground level of the housing blocks. These facilities, together with a kindergarten and a series of foot and bicycle paths linking the housing to the public transport stop, are designed to ensure that this well-conceived estate will not become an isolated island development.

Since this is social housing, the overwhelming majority of the inhabitants will come from the immediate area, thereby reducing the social tensions often formed when *Wessies* and *Ossies* meet.

ADDRESS Kastanienallee 47–49, Berlin-Pankow [P-17]
CLIENT Immobilienfund Winkelwiesen GbR
ARCHITECTS Schattauer + Tibes (masterplan and 156 housing units);
Liepe + Steigelmann (80 units); Elbe + Kalepky (90 units); Thomas
Schindler (100 units)
STRUCTURAL ENGINEER Ing. Gesellschaft G Pichler
BUS 122, 155
ACCESS open

Schattauer + Tibes (masterplan) 1994

Schattauer + Tibes (masterplan) 1994

Karow Nord

German reunification has released the same forces that have led to urban sprawl in the United States and elsewhere. Demand for housing is acute, East Germans will no longer accept the standard of housing available under Communism, and many West Berliners wish to escape the increasing crime and dirt of the city. The flight to the suburbs has begun. The problem is, there are no suburbs. Thus, on every square metre of property which is in undisputed ownership (free of restitution claims), housing is being constructed, mostly in small developments of between 20 and 50 units, with no attempt being made at integration with existing villages.

Moore Ruble Yudell's masterplan for Karow is an attempt to control these forces and channel them in a positive direction. To integrate 5000 new housing units with an existing small village is a difficult task in itself, but the new development also needs schools, shops, sports facilities and public green spaces.

The masterplan breaks down the development into separate neighbourhoods, linked with each other by streets, pedestrian ways and parks. Each neighbourhood is given its own identity through the public squares, the density and height of the units, and the street layout.

Several firms have been given the task of designing individual buildings, schools and sports facilities. Unfortunately, the architectural quality of the built housing is disappointing. Most buildings are simple, rendered blockwork cubes with holes punched in the façades in various patterns and formats and with only the roof forms helping to distinguish one from another. Even the colours were predetermined by the masterplan; the individual architects had little control. The opposite is true of the kindergartens and schools. Here the architects have each delivered fine works. The primary school by Liepe and Steigelmann is of particular interest.

Moore Ruble Yudell (masterplan) 1995–97

Moore Ruble Yudell (masterplan) 1995–97

Taken as a whole, the masterplan has been successful in breaking down the building volume into recognisable neighbourhoods and streets. Great attention was also given by the landscape architects to the integration of green spaces and water elements into the development, creating a very picturesque result.

ADDRESS Karower Chaussee, Achillesstraße, Berlin-Weissensee [IV-G2]
SIZE 98 hectares
S-BAHN Karow
BUS 158
ACCESS open

Moore Ruble Yudell (masterplan) 1995–97

Moore Ruble Yudell (masterplan) 1995–97

Competitions

SPREEBOGEN (Axel Schultes and Charlotte Frank – in planning)
A well-documented competition, which the local architect Axel Schultes deservedly won with an outstanding entry. Its clarity is devastating, its abstraction seductive. The most 'Berlin' of entries, it slices through the very element that divides East from West in order to tie them together.

The competition was only for 'ideas' and did not entitle Schultes to build. Instead, his proposal was used as a guideline for actual 'building' competitions in the area, which were intended to make up the various parts of his plan. As it turned out, the team of Schultes and Frank only just won the building competition for the chancellor's offices (now under construction), with the Alsenblock and Dorotheenblock going to others.

How this will affect the overall concept and appearance remains to be seen, but experience shows that the power and integrity of the original concept are usually compromised. Already their proposals for buildings east of the Luisenstraße seem to have been cut, and their design for the development of the blocks on the north bank of the Spree has been ignored in the current planning.

It is a pity that such a convincing project will not be built as planned. Instead, politicians and other nabobs will have succeeded in bastardising yet another work of art.

ADDRESS Platz der Republik, Berlin-Tiergarten [P–10]
S-BAHN Lehrter Stadtbahnhof
BUS 100

ALSENBLOCK (Stephan Braunfels)
Using Axel Schultes' competition result, a 'building' competition was held for the office block north of the Reichstag. The winning entry proposed jumping the Spree with part of its scheme to allow for its sheer density.

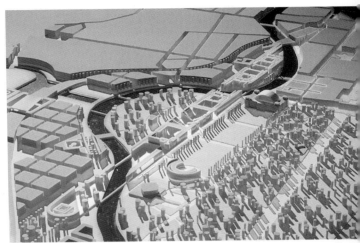

Axel Schultes

This idea is in keeping with Schultes' original concept and solves the problem of the fourth corner defined by the west block, the Reichstag and the Dorotheenblock. How well the architecture will react with the planned Kanzleramt and Dorotheenblock remains to be seen.

Its survival in its current form at all is in doubt; politicians are already discussing elimination of the overhanging western porch. It is feared that the resulting building will be a cannibalised version of the original design.
ADDRESS P Löbe-Straße/Schiffbauerdamm, Berlin-Tiergarten/
Berlin-Mitte [P–10]
S-BAHN Unter den Linden
BUS 100, 147

DOROTHEENBLOCK (Busmann & Haberer; de Architekten Cie; Schweger + Partner; Thomas van den Valentyn; von Gerkan, Marg und Partner)
The proposal for this area directly behind the Reichstag was complicated by two factors: the integration of the three remaining historical structures with the new, and the integration of the new with the rear fire walls of the planned buildings of the Pariser Platz.

The architects selected for the project have come up with a straight-forward yet clever solution. To solve the second problem, they would implement the same solution as that used for the buildings at Pariser Platz (see page 190), creating a series of courtyards that would provide light and air to the offices. The first problem would be solved by continuing this idea but breaking the edge along the river into a series of small blocks, in keeping with the size of the former Reichstagspräsidentenpalais.

Again the question raised is how the various projects will appear once juxtaposed with each other. More worrying is the question of how or in what form the project will survive the many funding cuts.

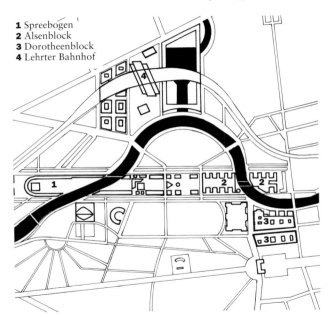

1 Spreebogen
2 Alsenblock
3 Dorotheenblock
4 Lehrter Bahnhof

ADDRESS Dorotheenstraße/Luisenstraße, Berlin-Mitte [P-10]
S-BAHN Unter den Linden
BUS 100
STATUS ground cleared

LEHRTER BAHNHOF AND ENVIRONS (station – von Gerkan, Marg und Partner; north area – Max Dudler; south area – Professor O M Ungers + Partner

The original Lehrter Bahnhof was once the most beautiful train station in Berlin. Although repairable after the war, it was demolished and the surrounding area left to rot. With the building of the Wall, the small train station at Zoo was used as the new main station in West Berlin and was capable of handling the few trains that still ran.

Since reunification, the debate concerning a new central station began in earnest. Although the former East Station (renamed Hauptbahnhof under the DDR) is large enough to accommodate the current traffic, it was decided to build a huge expensive station that would also accommodate the new magnet-powered Transrapid.

The design envisages the new station intersecting the existing elevated s-Bahn station. Most of the new tracks would be located underground, transversing the city north–south. The entire complex would be of steel and glass, with the crossing point forming an enormous atrium.

The immediate vicinity has also been subject to competition, with megalomaniac designs winning top prizes. Whether the money or the need for such a programmatic volume will be found is open to question.

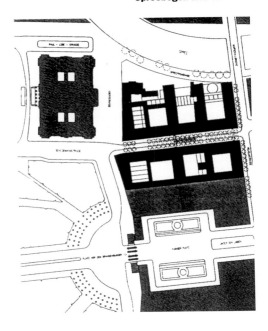

NEUES MUSEUM EXTENSION (Giorgio Grassi)

As part of the world famous Museumsinsel, the New Museum was built by Friedrich Stüler in 1843–55. Adjacent to the Nationalgalerie, it remains war-damaged to this day – forlorn, forgotten and neglected.

An invited competition for an extension was held in 1994 and Giorgio Grassi's entry was awarded first prize. When, however, Frank Gehry's submission arrived late (his studio had suffered earthquake damage), his conglomeration of crashing shapes and forms succeeded in unleashing a stormy debate among the jury members. The museum directors, who avidly support Gehry, have submitted a list of changes to Grassi which has made it almost impossible now not to accept Gehry's scheme.

Grassi's approach is one of minimal intervention; Gehry's proposal positively explodes. Grassi is low key; Gehry is an exhibitionist. Grassi is serious; Gehry is playful.

Many say that German architects analyse everything to such an extent that they cannot accept anything which does not have a deep symbolic meaning, no matter how boring. Here is a test case. Gehry's proposal is without question superior and the museum directors agree.

The debate, however, remains academic since the government does not have enough money to repair the existing structure, let alone put up a new building.

ADDRESS Bodestraße, Berlin-Mitte [Q–10]
S-BAHN Hackescher Markt
BUS 100, 157

DEUTSCHES HISTORISCHES MUSEUM EXTENSION (I M Pei)

The appointment of I M Pei as designer of an extension to the German History Museum is a move that has upset certain architectural circles in

Competitions

Frank O Gehry

Berlin. In the past all major public buildings were subject to an architectural competition, which before 1989 were for the most part open to all. Recently, however, most competitions have been limited, and the selected architects seem to be the same every time.

Pei's record speaks for itself. The JFK Library, the East Wing of the National Gallery in Washington, and the Pyramid in the courtyard of the Louvre are all highly popular and successful.

The museum is to be located directly behind the historical Zeughaus, an almost unnoticed and forgotten area. It is hoped that this project will help repair and revitalise this important part of Berlin.

ADDRESS Hinter dem Zeughaus, Berlin-Mitte [Q–10]
S-BAHN Friedrichstraße
BUS 100

LUSTGARTEN (Gerhard Merz (artist) with Professor O M Ungers)
The competition proposed separating the Lustgarten from the street and its heavy traffic to form a quiet oasis. However, this in no way reflected the area's history, for originally the street did not run through the Lustgarten but was stopped by an small extension of the Stadtschloß. The resulting space was thus bounded by the Altes Museum, the Berliner Dom, the Stadtschloß and the river's edge.

Luckily, public outcry prevented the implementation of the competition proposal, nicknamed 'the bus stop'. This project proved just how blind to reality and common sense many of today's leading architectural theoreticians can be.

ADDRESS Karl-Liebknecht-Straße, Berlin-Mitte [Q–10]
S-BAHN Hackescher Markt
BUS 100

1 Neues Museum extension
2 Deustches Historisches
  Museum extension
3 Lustgarten
4 Spreeinsel
5 Bauakademie

SPREE INSEL (Bernd Niebuhr)

Berlin was founded on an island between two 'fingers' of the River Spree, the so-called Spreeinsel (Spree Island). Today, north of Unter den Linden, this island can still be recognised in its original form, with its magnificent collection of museums creating a series of wonderful urban spaces.

However, the southern half is no longer recognisable as an island as such. Almost nothing remains of either the original street pattern or building substance. Heavily damaged during the war, the remains – including those of the Kaiser's palace – were demolished and a series of housing blocks erected. The Palast der Republik (the East German Parliament) was constructed on half of the original palace site, with the other half being used as a parade ground or car park. The offices of top government officials were located in the building forming the south edge of the car park and, with apt symbolism, the headquarters of the Socialist Unity Party were housed in Hitler's mint across the river.

An international ideas competition was held in 1993–94; more than 1000 hopefuls from 49 countries submitted proposals. The winner was to be determined mainly on what he or she would do with the Palast der Republik: incorporate it into a new composition, whip it down and build a modern replacement along the lines of the old palace, or rebuild the palace itself.

Local architect Bernd Niebuhr proposed a new rectangular media and conference centre, the size of the old Schloß. The oval interior courtyard would become a new public platz. South of this, he chose to recreate the historical urban setting of Schloßplatz. South of the Leipziger Straße and around the mint, he has been criticised for the density of building in the proposal. It is interesting to read the judges' comments; almost nowhere do they speak about the 'island', only about certain 'plätze'.

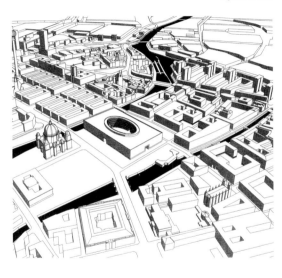

Bernd Niebuhr

The proposal to rebuild the old palace is documented on page 244. Niebuhr's proposal also contains neither a tower nor a cupola, the very elements that mark the turning point of various axes – a critical omission.

Nothing will be built in the near future, but it is well worth wandering through this area, visualising other possible solutions.

ADDRESS between Unter den Linden and Getraudenstraße, from Oberwasser Straße to Eastern Spree fork, Berlin-Mitte [R–10]
S-BAHN Alexanderplatz
U-BAHN Spittelmarkt

BAUAKADEMIE
This famous building by Karl Friedrich Schinkel survived the war and was actually under reconstruction when the DDR regime decided to stop work, tear it down, and build their own prestigious monument: the Ministry of Foreign Affairs. This large and extremely long building was recently torn down, and the chance now exists to rebuild Schinkel's masterpiece. However, no one can agree if it should be a total replica or a modern interpretation of the original. In addition, it is not clear what use it would have.

The city has no money available for a public museum or institute. Why new buildings for the Deutsches Institut für Bautechnik or the Deutsche Bauindustrie were built elsewhere when this site was free for development remains a mystery. Until agreement is reached, a green square will delineate the size of the building, and the green triangular platz in front is to be restored. Many feel that the rebuilding of Schinkel's masterpiece would be the thin edge of the wedge. If it is rebuilt, the Stadtschloß will follow.

ADDRESS Werder Straße, Berlin-Mitte [Q–10]
U-BAHN Hausvogteiplatz
BUS 147, 257

Karl Friedrich Schinkel

Index

Berlin: a guide to recent architecture

Berlin: a guide to recent architecture